The British
in
North Australia
1824-29:

Fort Dundas

Derek Pugh

The British in North Australia: Fort Dundas 1824-29

Text © Derek Pugh 2017

Original photographs © Derek Pugh 2017

Cover and Interior Design: Raven Tree Design

National Library of Australia Cataloguing-in-Publication entry :

Pugh, Derek, author.

Title: The British in North Australia : Fort Dundas 1824-29 / Derek Pugh.

ISBN: 9780992355869 (paperback)

Notes: Includes bibliographical references and index.

Subjects: Fortification--Northern Territory--Fort Dundas--History.

Convicts--Northern Territory--Fort Dundas--History.

Aboriginal Australians--Northern Territory--Melville

Island--Relations with British.

Tiwi (Australian people)--Relations with British.

Great Britian--Colonies--Administration--History.

Fort Dundas (N.T.)--Social conditions--History.

Melville Island (N.T.)--Social conditions--History

Also by Derek Pugh

Tambora : Travels to Sumbawa and the mountain that changed the world, 2014

Turn Left at the Devil Tree, 2013

Tammy Damulkurra, 1995 (2nd edition 2013)

The Owner's Guide to the Teenage Brain, 2011

Contact: *derekpugh1@gmail.com*

Website: *www.derekpugh.com.au*

"For Harry and Roy"

Contents

TABLE of ILLUSTRATIONS

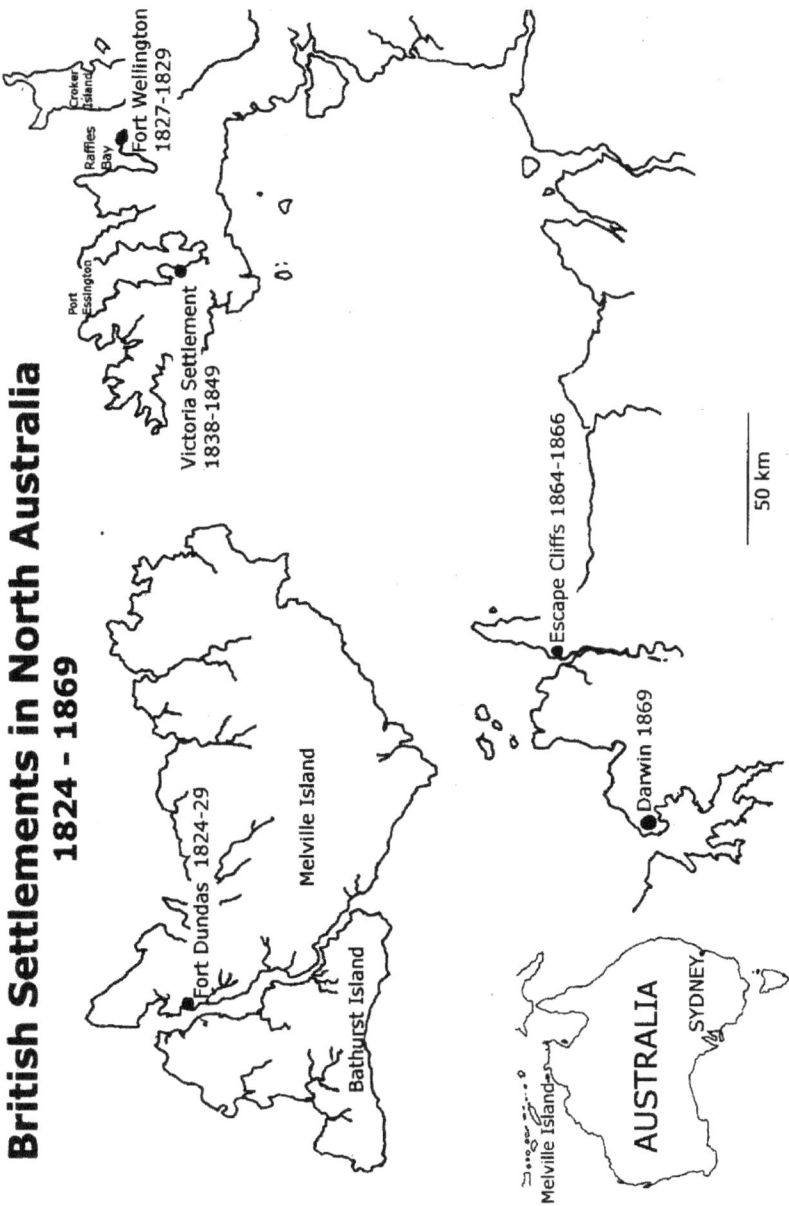

British Settlements in North Australia 1824 - 1869

Croker Island

Raffles Bay

Fort Wellington 1827-1829

Port Essington

Victoria Settlement 1838-1849

Fort Dundas 1824-29

Melville Island

Bathurst Island

Escape Cliffs 1864-1866

Darwin 1869

50 km

Melville Island

AUSTRALIA

SYDNEY

Map 1 British Settlements in North Australia 1824-29

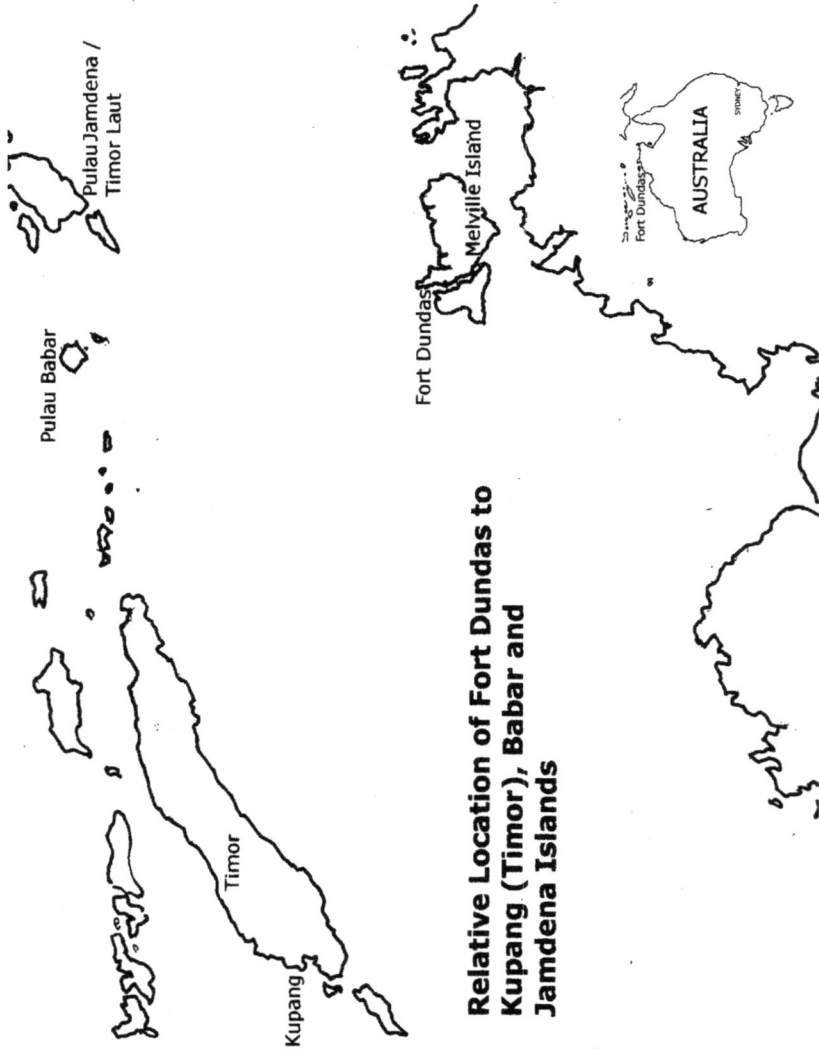

Map 2 Relative location of Fort Dundas to South East Asia.

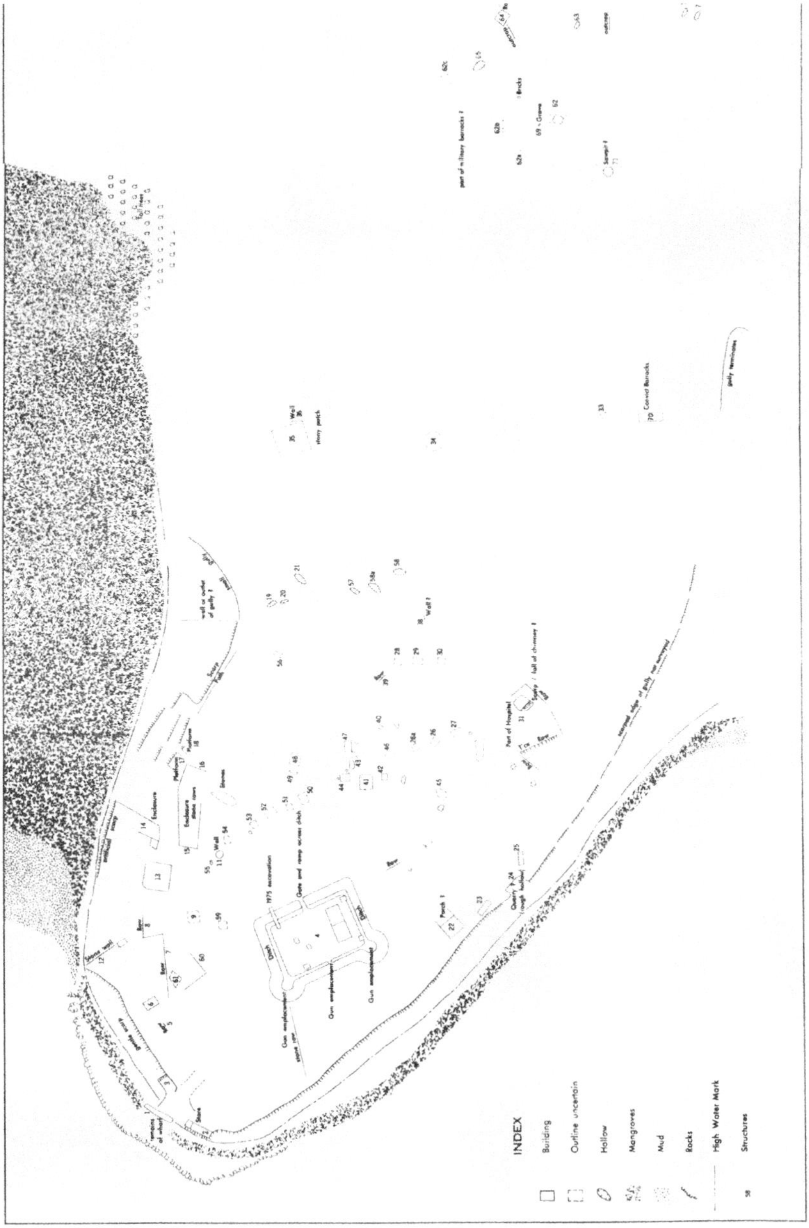

Map 3 A section of Eleanor Crosby's archaeological map of the Fort Dundas site, 1975

Acknowledgements

This research was assisted by the Northern Territory Government through the Northern Territory History Grants Program.

My thanks go to the numerous people who read the manuscript, or parts of it, and aided me by correcting errors, making edits, and encouraging me in the relentless research required. I particularly thank the following: Professor Alan Powell, Elizabeth Pugh, Dr Mark Heywood, Dr Peter Whelan, Jill Finch, Patrick Puruntatameri, Brett Jones, Michael Owen, and members of Darwin Authors Group. Thanks also to the amazing librarians at the Northern Territory Library (especially Margaret), the Mitchell Library, the State Libraries of South Australia and Western Australia, and the Charles Darwin University Library. Thanks to my family, Rina Yulia and our boys, Harry and Roy, who remained patient with me during the extended periods I was locked away with my computer.

Thanks lastly to the Tiwi people of Melville Island and particularly in Pirlangimpi, for their hospitality and generosity with their stories.

The Tiwi and other Indigenous people are notified that, as this is a history, it necessarily contains images and names of people who are deceased.

FOREWORD

Early in the nineteenth century the British tried to plant outposts on the Northern Territory coast. This proved to be the last burst of Imperial expansionism in Australia, designed to ensure that the whole of this great continent belonged to Britain alone and in hopes of generating trade from Asia. Now Derek Pugh's book completes the story of Fort Dundas, first and most significant of the outposts, for it set the pattern or all three (outposts). Here the soldiers, marines and convicts of the garrison struggled to survive against the hostility of the land, the climate, the native Tiwi people, and an isolation beyond our modern imagination. In clear and popular style, Derek Pugh tells the epic story of this gallant and ultimately misguided attempt to plant the first settlement on the wild coast of the future Northern Territory. It is truly an essential part of Territory and Australian history, which should be known to all.

Professor Alan Powell,
Emeritus Professor of History
Charles Darwin University.

PREFACE

Guarding the entrance to Apsley Strait, the treacherous Mermaid Shoals shield a channel of churning seawater that is pushed with incredible force between Bathurst and Melville Islands by huge tides. Passing through them under sail is fraught with difficulty, as ships can be propelled as much by the water as the wind.

In September 1824, three canvas-sailed ships appeared from the east and tentatively wove a path through the shoals to enter the strait. The lead swingers of *His Majesty's Ship Tamar* called the sea depth as the light winds eased her thirty-three metre hull slowly through the water. The tensions on board were palpable. Hitting a reef now when they were so close to their destination would be a disaster, and the charts, drawn only a few years previously by Phillip Parker King, were rudimentary to say the least. HMS *Tamar's* twenty-six gun ports were closed: there was no danger here from anything other than the reef.

On deck, Captain James Gordon Bremer could see the other two ships of his tiny fleet following him carefully through these unknown waters. The largest was the five-hundred ton freighter, *HMS Countess of Harcourt.* She outweighed the *Tamar* by nearly sixty tons and was now on her third voyage transporting convicts from the rotting hulks in England to the New Holland colonies. Captain George Bunn had been ordered to convey a party of marines, soldiers, volunteer convicts, and everything a new settlement would need north to the very top of New Holland before he returned to England.

The third member of the fleet was *HMS Lady Nelson*. This little brig was already famous. Designed and built in 1798, she carried three centreboard keels which, when lifted, allowed her to sail in waters a little less than two meters deep. She was the first ship to sail through Bass Strait in 1800 and was Lieutenant Murray's transport when he discovered Port Phillip in 1801. She was also part of Matthew Flinders's little fleet as a support for the *Investigator* during his circumnavigation of the continent. Flinders never liked her, and when she hit a reef near Port Macquarie and lost one of her keels, she was sent back to Sydney. She then spent years supporting Norfolk Island and helped in the settling of Port Macquarie and Tasmania. By 1824, she was an elderly lady, with twenty-four years of service to the colony behind her. Much smaller than the other ships in Bremer's fleet at sixteen metres, weighing only sixty tons, she was crewed by just nine or ten sailors. The *Lady Nelson* would be based at the new northern outpost and make supply runs to the East Indies, to ensure the settlement remained well provisioned and the settlers well fed and healthy. Captain Samuel Johns no doubt was looking forward to his role in helping the pioneers of the settlement create what they believed would become a new Singapore. There was no way he could have guessed the tragic fate of his ship, the entire crew, and himself a few weeks later.

The fleet anchored together in calm water off Luxmore Head, twenty or more kilometres down the strait. Small parties were sent in several directions in the ship's boats and by foot on shore to look for water. Captain Bremer himself found it by sinking waist deep in marshy ground as he stalked a waterbird with his musket. With fresh water, they had what they needed, and within days, the convicts and stores were unloaded onto a nearby point and work begun on what was the first British settlement in New Holland north of the Tropic of Capricorn.

Founded with high optimism, the settlement lasted for a little over four years—from September 1824 until February 1829. Most considered it a failure, and it is little known nowadays, but it did achieve one of the aims of the British Admiralty of the time—claiming ownership of Northern Australia. It was named by Bremer on 21 September 1824, an auspicious date only because it is also Trafalgar Day, and some of the men there were veterans of the battle. In its short existence we have tales of great privation, survival, battles with the indigenous Tiwi tribes, greed, kidnapping, piracy, slavery, murder, scurvy, and also the first wedding and birth of a European child in Northern Australia.

1

LONDON 1823

A new colony is a massive undertaking for any government. It requires people of vision, willing to drive the idea and the huge effort and expense that is required. Fort Dundas and the other northern settlements in New Holland were no exception. The initial drivers of the idea in 1823 were men who championed it from two completely different standpoints. The first was a trader, Captain William Barns, who saw the settlement's commercial value, and the second was a senior government strategist, John Barrow, who focused on its political and military value. Both lobbied the government in London for a settlement, specifically through Earl Bathurst, Secretary of State for War and the Colonies.

Captain Barns had some experience in the East Indies: he had arrived in Sydney on 15 January 1822, in command of the *Minstrel*, a 351-ton merchant ship he had brought out from England. The *Minstrel* carried twenty or so free passengers, including several families, who were dropped off in Hobart the previous December, along with a huge range of merchandise soon advertised in the Hobart Town

Gazette: everything from clothing to cheese cutters, beaver-skin gloves, and artificial flowers.

Barns had quickly moved on to Sydney with further trade goods to sell. He stayed there only a month, as he was keen to seek out more business in the East Indies archipelago north of New Holland. In Sydney, Governor Macquarie had been replaced by Governor Brisbane the previous December, and his homebound ship spent time waiting inside 'The Heads' to leave Sydney on the same tide as the *Minstrel,* on 15 February 1822. Macquarie mentioned the *Minstrel* in his journal and was sure it was headed for whaling grounds. However, Barns was actually heading to Penang via Cape York to trade, and over the next two years* he established and ran a trade route between the Moluccas and Sydney.

Back in London in 1823, although primarily a trader, Barns was the man who seemed to have most convinced Earl Bathurst of the need for a new settlement on the northern coast of New Holland. He explained that a British port in the Gulf of Carpentaria would open the Indies Archipelago from Timor to the Solomon Islands to the 'British Flag.' He told Bathurst that it was '… hardly possible to describe in the Limits of a Letter the benefits that are likely to accrue from a Settlement in these parts' and requested and received a personal interview with him[12].

Barns's enthusiasm was persuasive. His interests were not only patriotic, but commercial, because he had been suffering what he considered to be severe discrimination as a foreign trader in the Indies, which were Dutch possessions. Barns had been 'warned off' under threat of seizure at Amboina in the Moluccas in May 1822, and he had been stung by the heavy Dutch tariffs in Moluccan ports. He sought sympathy when he reported a 'disgraceful abuse of the British Flag on the part of the Dutch Government against the natives of the Molucca Islands.' He also claimed that the Dutch were determined to exclude all rivals from the region's trade and may already have had plans to

---

* A number of sources say four years, but the recorded dates indicate two years only—1822 and 1823.

set up a trading post on New Holland shores, to access the Macassan trepang (*beche-de-mer*) industry which, he exaggerated, was worth £180,000 per annum (in modern terms, approximately $35 million).

Barns had some powerful backers. George Larpent, the chairman of the London-based East India Trade Committee, was easy to convince. Barns, Larpent, and the committee members, some of whom employed Barns at one time or another, could see great opportunities for trade in the East Indies and northern New Holland in coffee, trepang, pearl shell, sandalwood, tortoise shell, and spices such as nutmeg. But if all these areas were allowed to fall under a Dutch or a French sphere of influence, the opportunities would be lost to Britain. They felt that a British, free port in northern New Holland would overtake Batavia's significance in the region, and that it was a natural extension of the British sphere of influence, with an inestimable value.

The second proponent of the settlement, John Barrow[†], was the Second Secretary of the Admiralty. Barrow was already concerned that the British claim to the whole of New Holland seemed tenuous at best. He knew that the northern coasts were more accessible to the Indies than they were to Sydney, and in a letter to the Undersecretary of State for War and the Colonies, Sir Robert Wilmot Horton, he explained:

> *"From the neighbouring island of Timor, it is but a step to the northern parts of New Holland; and it would be well to bear in mind that they would have a justifiable plea, in planting an establishment on any part of the Northern Coast of the latter, in our own example of taking possession of the Eastern Coast and Island of Van Diemen, the original discovery of which by the Dutch is not disputed. Indeed I believe it is admitted... that Occupancy is a stronger title than priority of discovery: but be this as it may, in the present instance our own conduct may be quoted against us."[14]*

† John Barrow was later a founder of the Royal Geographical Society.

Barrow knew that William Barns and the East India Trade Committee were petitioning for a settlement during 1823 and the early months of 1824, but commerce was secondary to him. He saw the importance of geography, and his plan was to ensure Britain retain dominance over the whole of New Holland by placing small military outposts around its shores. These military outposts would have high strategic importance and would legally ensure Britain's claim was well established before the Dutch, French, or anyone else could make a claim. In the end, four military outposts were established during the 1820s through his influence: Fort Dundas, Fort Wellington, Western Port, and King George Sound.

Earl Bathurst and the British government had been presented with much food for thought. Phillip Parker King had recently returned from surveying the north coast of New Holland, where he had charted and named Cobourg Peninsula, Port Essington, and the Tiwi Islands (Bathurst and Melville), and he spoke and wrote of the area in glowing terms. Bathurst consulted King, who recommended Port Essington as a suitable site for the settlement. King's surveys were yet to be published, and there was concern that, once they were, there would be a rush from the Netherlands to claim the area as their own, so there was a need for speed. The decision was made in a matter of months: there would be a 'second Singapore' with the establishment of a new trading port on the north coast of New Holland and Britain would thus maintain sovereignty over the whole of the vast island continent they had claimed.

The man they found to put their plan into place was an experienced naval officer named Captain James John Gordon Bremer.

2

SYDNEY 1824

Sir James John Gordon Bremer was a career naval officer. Born in 1786, he entered the navy at the age of eight. He was a young lieutenant at the Battle of Trafalgar in 1805, and he distinguished himself there by his role in the capture of the French ship, *De Weser*. He was appointed captain in 1815, and was thus already an experienced commander by February 1824, when Earl Bathurst ordered him to take command of the *Tamar** and sail from England to the north coast of New Holland via Sydney. He was to establish *two* military settlements on the north coast of New Holland, using his discretion to choose suitable sites that would allow the British to lay claim to the northern coast and to break the trade monopoly held in that area by the Dutch. It was suggested that one settlement be

Figure 1 Captain James John Gordon Bremer.

---

*   For a full list of the crew of the Tamar see Ennis 1825 p302 made on either of the Tiwi Islands and the other at Port Essington on the Cobourg Peninsula. The mouth of the Liverpool River, where Maningrida stands today, was mentioned as an alternative.

Phillip Parker King had named one of the Tiwi Islands *Bathurst* during his survey of the coast in 1818. History doesn't record Bathurst's emotions at this honour or its influence, if any, on his decision six years later to order the northern settlement on, or near, there, but the settlers on Melville Island only had to look out across the narrow Apsley Strait to remember who authorised their existence in this remote part of the world. King named Melville Island after the First Lord of the Admiralty, Viscount Melville, whose name was Robert Dundas. Although he never had much to do with Australia's development, Robert Dundas received the double honour of having a fort named after him on an island named after his title. Ironically, Henry Dundas, Robert's father, was one of Bathurst's main political foes in the struggle to abolish slavery. He was also the London based supervisor of the 'Battle of the Hawkesbury' in New South Wales, where British soldiers fought against warriors of the Dharuk tribe[64].

Bremer carried his orders to Governor Brisbane, then in charge of New South Wales:

> *"My Lords, I am commanded to signify to you His Majesty's pleasure that a Ship of War should be dispatched without delay to the North West Coast of New Holland, for the purpose of taking formal possession, in the name of His Majesty, of that part of the said Coast contained between the western Shore of Bathurst Island and the eastern side of Cobourg Peninsula, including the whole of Bathurst and Melville Islands, and the said Peninsula."* [16]

The establishment of settlements by the British in the region wasn't new. The East India Company had tried several times, the first at Fort Coronation at Dore Bay in West Papua in 1793 and at Balambangan, off Borneo in 1803. These had both failed after two years, but Singapore, a settlement started in 1819, was looking more successful as business was booming. Singapore enthralled the Admiralty. Barrow had said that it had 'risen like an enchantment,' and a second success like that would mean a great boost to Britain's fortunes in the area[16].

The *Tamar* carried twenty-six guns and was originally a warship, launched in 1814, during the Napoleonic Wars. On her maiden voyage, she had been sent to Halifax, Nova Scotia, but was quickly struck by tragedy as seventy-five men, including the captain, died of fever. Now, under Bremer's command, the *Tamar* arrived in Sydney in June 1824, and Bremer spent a few weeks in preparation for the northern settlement. For legal reasons, any convicts sent north had to be volunteers because the new settlement was outside the longitude mentioned in the act that established New South Wales as a penal colony. Also, to improve the chance of success, it was decided that they should be skilled workers, and advertisements went up very soon after Bremer's arrival to find such men.

Many convicts may have been keen to go, and it is possible that more volunteered than were accepted, but they needed to have skills that would be of use to the settlement, and they were screened by the government in Sydney. Their inducement was a ticket-of-leave after only a year's service, which was a valuable item. Forty-five convict volunteers were accepted for the initial expedition. They were carpenters, stonemasons, brick makers, bricklayers, plasterers, nail-makers, a plumber, servants, a glazier, and others[*].

Bremer also wanted free settlers to join them, so he placed advertisements in the *NSW Gazette* to attract them:

> *"…passage and Provisions found them by the Government, and be allowed Rations for six months after their arrival, provided for the half of that period they devote their Services to the Crown."*[70]

He may have been underwhelmed—only three skilled free 'mechanics'

---

[*] See Appendix 3 for a list of trades and occupations of all Fort Dundas convicts.

7

signed up: William Potter, nail-maker and blacksmith; Henry Feathers, bricklayer; and Edward Chapman, sawyer. They would receive double pay for their efforts.

Bremer was anxious to get going, not only for the adventure of founding the new settlement, but also because the winds would be shifting eastwards later in the year, and he was to sail on to India once the settlement was established. His orders allowed him to take command of any Vessel of War stationed in New South Wales to aid him, but none was available, but he did manage to secure a convict transport ship, the *Countess of Harcourt*, and a small tender named the *Lady Nelson*.

The *Countess of Harcourt* was originally a merchant ship launched at Prince of Wales Island in 1812. She was sold to the British government

VIEW of the LADY NELSON in the THAMES.
This Plate is respectfully Dedicated to Capt. John Schanck. of the Royal Navy by his obedient Servant J. Grant, Lieut. R.N.

Figure 2 His Majesty's Ship Lady Nelson was stationed at Port Cockburn to carry out supply runs to Timor. She was captured and sunk by pirates on Babar Island in 1824, which caused great shortages at Fort Dundas. A replica nowadays sails out of Hobart.

in 1814, and was involved in several skirmishes, including being captured by an American privateer later in the same year, but she was recaptured in 1815.

The *Countess* made five trips transporting convicts to Australia, starting in 1821, under the command of George Bunn. On her first trip, she sailed from Portsmouth on 19 April 1821, and arrived in Hobart on 27 July, with 172 male convicts. This was the quickest journey to the colony ever made, ninety-nine days, and it remained a record until 1837. In comparison, the First Fleet had taken 252 days.

On her second voyage as a convict transporter, she also carried an officer and thirty other ranks from the 3rd Regiment of Foot (the 'Buffs') working as the guards. Some of these men became part of the detachment to Fort Dundas when the *Countess* came back to Sydney on her third trip, transporting convicts, with more Buffs guarding them, in 1824. On arrival in Sydney on this trip, Captain Bunn was ordered to join the *Tamar* for the journey north to transport the convict volunteers and most of the soldiers and marines, plus up to eighteen months of supplies for the commissariat. The *Countess* was then to return to England.

The small *Lady Nelson* also carried marines, or soldiers, and supplies, but she was to be based at the new settlement to trade for supplies in the East Indies.

The little fleet set sail on 24 August 1824, under Bremer's command, and headed north to Torres Strait before turning west towards Port Essington, reaching there on 20 September 1824. According to *The Monthly Magazine,* the *Tamar* was the largest warship yet to navigate the dangerous shoals of northern New Holland [90]

3

MELVILLE ISLAND 1824

"… and then Mudangkala, the old blind woman arose from the ground carrying three babies in her arms. As she crawled in the darkness across the featureless landscape, seawater followed and filled the imprints made by her body. Eventually the pools became one and formed a channel. The old woman continued on her journey overland and once again the moulded earth filled with the flow of water. Before she left, Mudangkala covered the islands with plants and filled the land and sea with living creatures. Finally the land was prepared for her children and for generations of children who followed." [136]

In London, the original orders had told Bremer to establish two settlements in the north, but he was under-resourced and wisely decided to establish only one fortified outpost. He would leave it under the command of an officer provided for that purpose by Governor Brisbane. Earl Bathurst had stipulated that:

> "… *wherever the first Settlement be established, it is highly important that formal possession be taken of, and His Majesty's Colours hoisted upon each of the three points mentioned herein, the Naval Commander's attention therefore has been particularly drawn to this point.*" [16]

Port Essington is a huge natural harbour several times larger than Sydney's Port Jackson. When the fleet arrived, Bremer formally unfurled the Union Jack on Point Record and took possession of the land stretching west from Cape York to 129°E longitude, in the name of King George IV. Lieutenant John Septimus Roe scattered some coins and buried a bottle there containing a copy of the possession documents. Roe had sailed as an officer with Phillip Parker King on the *Mermaid* during his surveys of the coast, so he had been sought out to work for Bremer on the *Tamar* as the most experienced officer available. He was an intelligent man destined for great things in a long career, eventually as the surveyor general for the founding of Perth in Western Australia.

Whilst on Point Record, someone found a small well, little more than a hole fenced with bamboo, which contained a small quantity of thick water. Bremer recognised the work of the 'Malays' as, he confidently claimed, the bamboo was not native to New Holland. Unfortunately, the well contained too little water to be a resource for a new settlement, so small parties went out in small boats and on foot to search for a fresh water creek or billabong that would be more useful.

An accident marred the search:

> "*A boat belonging to the Countess of Harcourt, returning to the ship, with twelve persons on board, upset, but was happily discovered from*

the Tamar; and, by the great exertions of Lieutenant Golding, eight of them were saved. Two soldiers of the 3rd regiment, the Captain's steward of the Harcourt, and a fine lad, the son of a clergyman, an apprentice, were unfortunately drowned." * [52]

After a few days without finding water, the fleet moved on to Melville Island, landing on Luxmore Head, where Roe had been before with Captain King. Bremer officially took possession of it, 'with the same ceremonies and salutes as at Port Essington,' on 26 September 1824, and the next day sent Lieutenant Roe to Bathurst Island to take possession of that island as well:

> *"…the Declaration read aloud to my boat's crew, and all the noise 8 persons were capable of making was called into action in giving 9 cheers to crown our undertaking." (Roe, letter to father, 1824)*

On Melville Island, they then set about searching for water again, and this time quickly had more luck. A permanent billabong and stream just inland from a beach in the Apsley Strait was found:

> *"Tuesday 28th: Captain Bremer, while shooting in marshy ground, fell up to his middle in water, which upon tasting, he found fresh, and a running stream: weighed anchor about three o'clock and went further down the bay, to a place where Captain Bremer had found the fresh water, and where he now determined to fix the settlement: anchored then in a well sheltered bay, with deep water almost to the shore."* [133]

The convicts and stores were brought ashore two days later and work started. The convicts were ordered to fell trees and clear land,

---

* Privates Edward Oakly and Joseph Churchill, plus a steward and ship's boy (the apprentice), were drowned. Of the survivors, one was Assistant Surgeon Turner, the Assistant Surgeon to the colony and an officer named Mills of the *Tamar*.

and within a few more days, they started building the fort itself using the felled timber. After three weeks, on 21 October 1824, the anniversary of the Battle of Trafalgar, one bastion of the fort was complete, and Bremer lined up the soldiers and convicts, ordered the marines to hoist the Union Jack, and fired a Royal Salute with the two 9-pounder cannons. Then he formally named the bay in front of them King Cove, the harbour Port Cockburn, and the fort itself, Fort Dundas.

The settlers' very first interactions with the local people, the Tiwi, were made during the eight weeks Bremer was at the settlement. Always suspicious of each other, Bremer, nevertheless, felt the early meetings were satisfactory, but within a few weeks, they degenerated into violence (see Chapter 8).

Descriptions of the events and the fort were sold to *The Sydney Gazette* within months. Public interest in the settlement was high in Sydney, and officers who could write well could make extra income from providing the information. They wrote anonymously because they were not permitted to publish official journals. Newspapers quoted two major anonymous writers*, calling them the *Gentleman in Command* and the *Anonymous Officer*. They give interesting accounts of the first weeks of the settlement:

> *"The pier, having been finished on the 21st, the party employed on that service, and the whole strength of the expedition was directed to the fort, and completing the different works of the Settlement. Second of November, commenced building a magazine; on the 7th, Commissariat store-house was finished; and by the 8th, the whole of the provisions, stores, and necessaries, were landed from the Harcourt, and properly secured therein: this storehouse is built of wood, well thatched, and is fully equal to the occasion, until a more regular, and substantial one can be built; it contains nearly eighteen months provisions, &c, for the Colony. The fort, which commands the whole anchorage (the shot from it reaching across*

---

* By a process of elimination, Lieutenant Mills was probably either the *Anonymous Officer* and/or the *Gentleman in Command* who wrote for *The Sydney Gazette*.

to Bathurst Island,) was completed (with the exception of the ditch) on the 9th of November. It is composed of timber of great weight and solidity, in layers five feet in thickness at the base; the height of the work inside is six feet, surrounded by a ditch ten feet deep, and fifteen feet wide: on it are mounted two 9-pounder guns, and four 18-pounder carronades, with a 12-pounder boat gun to shift on occasion, and to be put on board the Lady Nelson, when it is necessary to detach her to the neighbouring

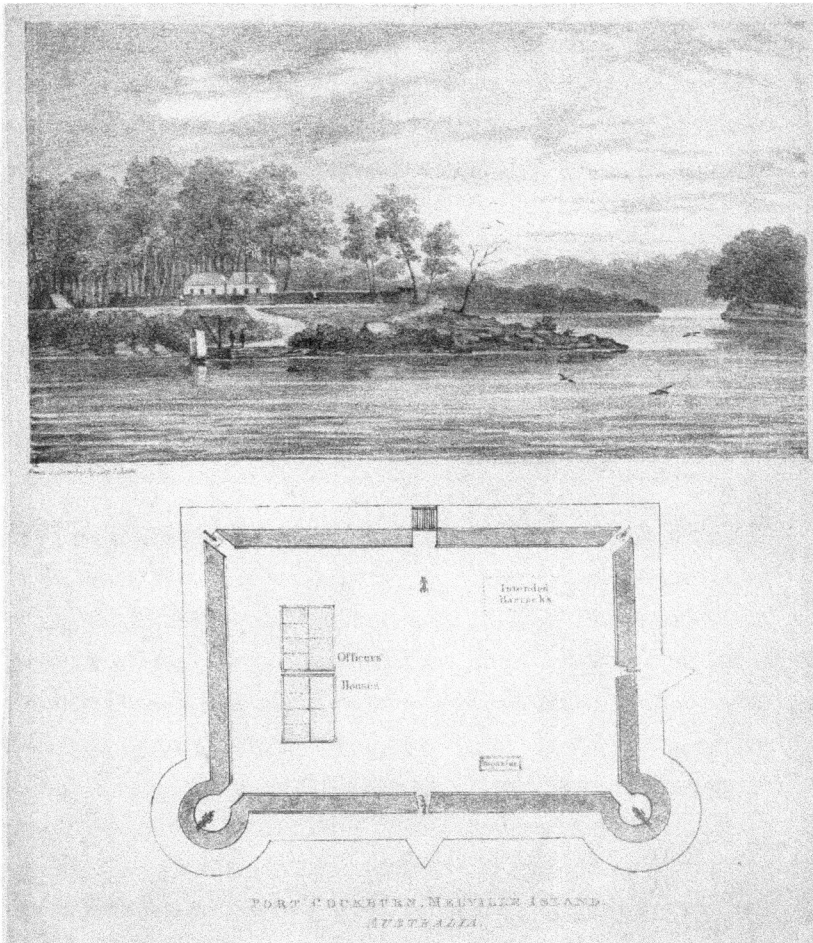

Figure 3 Port Cockburn sketch by Capt Bunn showing the commandant's and officers' houses within the fort's walls. The commissariat store is seen only as a dark roof behind the derrick. The small building in the centre is the blacksmith. Harris Island, on the right, is unrealistically close.

15

islands, or for other purposes. Those guns are provided with fifty rounds of round and grape, and are part of the upper-deck guns of this ship.

The fort is rectangular, its sides being seventy-five yards, by fifty; in this square are houses for the Commandant, and the officers of the garrison, and a barrack for the soldiers is to be put into immediate progress. The soldiers and convicts, have built themselves good and comfortable cottages near the fort. The climate of those islands, is one of the best that can be found, between the tropics; the thermometer rarely reaching eighty-eight; and in the morning, at dawn, sometimes falling to seventy-six; nothing can be more delightful than this part of the twenty-four hours. I was obliged, by necessity, with the whole of the ship's company, to be constantly exposed to a vertical sun, but fortunately few have suffered, and none very severely."

The gardens were started at Garden Point, about a kilometre from the fort, because that is where the best fresh water flowed and the soil looked most promising. To get there without a boat, a path was cut through the forest around the back of the mangroves that grew thickly on the inside of King Cove, and a small log bridge was built across the mud and water of a tidal creek.

"The soil of this island appears to be excellent. In digging a deep well for the use of the Settlement, we found a fine vegetable mould about two feet deep; then soft sand stone rock, occasionally mixed with strata of red clay, until the depth of thirty feet, when we came to a vein of yellow clay and gravel, through which an abundance of water instantly sprang, and rose to the height of six feet. It is probable that this soil is capable of producing most (if not all) the tropical fruits, and shrubs of the Eastern islands; the plants brought from Sydney, flourish luxuriantly; particularly the orange and lemon, the lime, banana, naval, and sugar cane; melons and pumpkins spring up immediately; and the maize was above ground on the fourth day after it was sown. We found the stream of water first discovered, to run into several large ponds near the beach, (which affords to ships an easy mode of watering), and no doubt valuable

rice plantations may be fostered in their neighbourhood. Amongst the trees, some of which are of noble growth, I found a sort of lignum vitae* *which probably will be valuable for block sheaves, and several others, which appear to be well calculated for naval purposes."* [134]

Figure 4 JS Roe's labelled sketch from Fort Dundas looking north towards Garden Point from November 1824. HMSs Tamar, Countess of Harcourt and Lady Nelson are shown. The blacksmith's roof and the store (commissariat) can be seen along the coastline. (Courtesy State Library of Western Australia)

The enthusiasm practically oozes out of this writing. The new settlers were excited to be there. Sydney Town was only thirty-six years old, so perhaps they imagined growth on Melville Island would be as successful and they were full of pioneer spirit.

Lieutenant Roe, who was only on Melville Island for eight weeks, made several sketches of the new fort, and wrote about it in glowing terms in long letters to his father:

"With amazing spirit and perseverance and laborious undertaking a wide piece of land of the nature of Point Barlow, under the burning heat of a vertical sun, proceeded with great rapidity; and as soon as sufficient space was cleared a fort was marked out, 75 yards in length by 50 wide, and our seamen and marines commenced erecting its parapets with the heavy trunks of trees as they were felled while the

---

* *Lignum vitae* is Latin for "tree of life." It was a term used for hard wood that can be harvested to make tools such as mallets, blocks, etc. On Melville Island, the writer is probably referring to the Australian Ironwood *Erythrophleum chlorostachys.*

17

other party ran out a ... substantial wharf to the low water mark, another dug a deep well near the fort & others commenced sawing planking, erecting huts, a commissariat store... and as fast as possible all the stores were landed from the Countess of Harcourt."[115]

A pale and evocative watercolour painting of Fort Dundas, as viewed from the other side of King Cove, is held in the National Library of Australia and attributed to the naturalist, soldier, and artist, Charles Hamilton Smith(see figure 5). If Smith was the artist, it would have been painted after his retirement and may have been imagined from the sketches of others because there is no evidence of Smith being at the fort at the same time as the *Tamar* and the *Lady Nelson*, both of which are depicted. The painting shows the low walls of the fort and two prefabricated buildings within it.

Figure 5 Fort Dundas watercolour attributed to Charles Hamilton Smith, 1824. Both HMS Tamar (right) and HMS Lady Nelson are depicted. The commissariat building stands next to the dock (Courtesy: National Library of Australia)

The *Tamar* was in Port Cockburn for eight weeks in the 'build-up' months of October and November before the wet season. The days were hot and humid, almost without rain, and it was a time of year when even the most ardent adventurer's optimism might wilt. However, Bremer's enthusiasm for the place never faltered. His orders required him to stay at the settlement to 'afford them countenance and protection so long as may appear to him and the Senior Officer in Charge of the said settlements to be necessary.'

No doubt with his mind also on the season and the fair winds he needed to sail to India, he felt that this needed only about eight weeks:

> *"On the 13th of November, the fort, wharf, soldiers' huts, officers' houses, and commissariat store being completed, also an excellent well, thirty feet deep and six in diameter, and the provisions all landed, Captain Bremer took his departure for India, leaving an officer and thirty marines to assist in the protection of the settlement. The establishment at this time was as follows: Captain Barlow and Lieutenant Everard, 3rd Regiment; Lieutenant Williamson, Royal Marines; Assistant-Surgeon Turner, Royal Artillery; Mr Miller, Commissariat Department; Mr. Tollemache, Commissariat Storekeeper; thirty soldiers of the Royal Marines; fifty of 3rd Regiment; and forty-five convicts. One small vessel of about sixty tons (the Lady Nelson) was also left for the purpose of fetching supplies from the Island of Timor."* [33]

So Bremer sailed on to India on the *Tamar*. He had stayed long enough to see the initial settlement established, and his reports to London were in such glowing terms that the Admiralty were encouraged. His career continued brightly and, despite the failure of Fort Dundas over the next few years, in part because of Bremer's poor choice of position, he was chosen again to establish the new settlement at Port Essington in 1838. He named this settlement Victoria after the new Queen. Like Fort Dundas, it also appeared to Bremer as a settlement of boundless opportunity, and he advocated the selling of land to permanent settlers and envisioned a flourishing British trade colony to rival all others. Victoria Settlement lasted longer than Fort Dundas, eleven years, but once again, Bremer's optimism was misplaced.

Bremer never returned to Australia after the Victoria Settlement was established. He was awarded a knighthood for his service to the crown, and he died in 1850 as a highly respected and decorated naval officer at home in England. Of his little fleet, the *Tamar* was used by the navy for a few more years, but in 1831, it was converted to a coal hulk at Plymouth and then sold for scrap in 1837. The *Countess of Harcourt*, which departed Fort Dundas at the same time as the *Tamar,* sailed to Mauritius and from there back to Britain with purser Henry Ennis carrying the first reports and dispatches about the settlement. She made two further trips to Australia, transporting convicts, before she was wrecked on the coast of Corfu in 1830. The third ship of the fleet, the *Lady Nelson,* stayed at the Fort as a supply ship, but pirates soon pillaged and burned her (see Chapter 9).

As Bremer sailed away from Fort Dundas in 1824, he was farewelled by the full complement of marines and soldiers who were now stationed there to continue building the colony. A young officer, Captain Maurice Barlow, who was initially as optimistic about their success as Bremer had been, was left in command of the new outpost.

4

BARLOW

The presence of a military garrison was a major justification for the existence of Fort Dundas. Even those interested in the commercial side of a new settlement believed that having a military presence would attract settlers, especially the Chinese, and the community would begin to flourish.

The NSW Corps had provided defence for the colony of New South Wales from 1790 until 1810, but the events of the 'Rum Rebellion' saw them disbanded and replaced with regular British Army regiments on a rotational basis. The first regiment to arrive in 1810, the 73rd, came with Governor Lachlan Macquarie. The second was the Northamptonshire Regiment, the 48th Regiment of Foot, who arrived in 1817. Then from 1824, the Royal East Kent Regiment, the 3rd Regiment of Foot, or the 'Buffs,' was the third regiment to be stationed in Australia. Of their number, twenty-four military personnel*, under the command of twenty nine year old Captain Maurice Barlow, were sent to Fort Dundas. The Buffs were one of the oldest regiments in the British army, dating back to 1572 (the title '3rd' meant that the regiment was third in order of precedence to the king).

---

*   See Appendix 2 for a list of the names of officers and men who are known.

Little is known about the individual Buffs who were stationed at Fort Dundas. Historian Peter Spillett travelled to England to find records of their names or further details of their lives, but failed to find any, even in the regimental museums. Unfortunately, the main record of who they were is a list of those that died during their Melville Island posting (see Appendix 4).

In 1821, the Buffs had started to travel to Australia in small detachments as prisoner escorts on convict ships. The regiment remained in Australia until 1827, in between the campaigns of the Napoleonic Wars and India, and they were divided into four detachments. The first three were based in Sydney (1821), Hobart (1822), and the 'Sydney Headquarters' (1823). Among other achievements twenty-four of the Buffs, with two officers, were brought together by Acting Governor William Stewart as the first company of Mounted Police in NSW, during his brief tenure in the position before the new Governor, Ralph Darling arrived in 1825.

Captain Barlow arrived in Sydney with the fourth detachment in 1824 to find that his men were to be spread across the colony to a number of different locations: specifically Port Dalrymple, Parramatta, Liverpool, Newcastle, Port Macquarie and Bathurst Town. Barlow had a good reputation in his regiment, and he was posted to Fort Dundas with his twenty-four men amid a wave of hasty optimism, tempered by the xenophobic concerns that the French or Dutch would get there first. It is likely he had no forewarning of his fate, and he was selected because he was on duty with a section of his regiment in Sydney when Bremer arrived needing soldiers and marines who could be spared by the Governor. There is no evidence that Barlow, the soldiers, or the marines were volunteers in any way, but rather they were quickly mustered together and ordered to go north with Bremer. Barlow may have initially been keen, because he was a young captain with little experience of command. He may have seen the posting as an opportunity worth taking. It all took just a few weeks to organise.

Managing a convict colony and a military garrison with the intention of turning it into a major trading port, whilst maintaining a military presence that was designed to deter the French or the Dutch from also settling, was a difficult task. But it was even more of a challenge because Barlow also had to cope with the potential cross-cultural difficulties arising after contact with the original inhabitants of the island, the Tiwi. Nevertheless, from his early reports, Captain Barlow was initially as enamoured by the prospects of Fort Dundas as Bremer had been. His first report reached London in April 1825 and he wrote:

> "... never was so promising a spot in a naval, commercial and agricultural point of view, as the two islands of Melville and Bathurst and the intervening strait. The soil and climate is so fine that there is not an article either in the Temperate or Torrid Zone that might not be raised... We may here therefore redeem what we have lost by our generosity to the Dutch. And I have no doubt, that in a commercial point of view, it will become another Singapore." [13]

Perhaps, at first, it seemed like a big adventure. After all, they were to build a new city to rival Singapore. If it had been a success, Maurice Barlow could now be as famous as Governor Phillip or Stamford Raffles. The *Sydney Gazette* said of him:

> "The Government of the little Colony was held in deserved estimation, as Captain Barlow is said to be 'plain and sincere in his manners; honourable and correct in his conduct; and anxious that everything in the settlement should be carried on in the simplest manner.'"[133]

But Barlow was ill-prepared for the assignment. He was a career soldier better suited to theatres of war, without the background or training necessary to establish a new colony.

Thus, with little knowledge, even of the requirements of a healthy diet and with an inexperienced Assistant Surgeon his only medical support, the settlement soon started to sicken around him, and the work output slowed. To make things worse the trade ships they expected to arrive never came.

Barlow was already known to his men in the 3rd Regiment, but at Fort Dundas, he was also in charge of the twenty-seven marines who had travelled with Bremer from England.

Even less is known about the Melville Island marines than the Buffs. They were the men who fired the volleys on Trafalgar Day as Bremer gave his speeches of provenance and named the surrounding landmarks after VIPs from the other side of the world. Their main job was to guard the convicts and build and man the fortifications of the fort. At Fort Dundas, where eventually even the convicts were permitted to walk around armed with muskets or pistols as protection against the Tiwi, 'guarding convicts' seems to have taken on a different meaning. The marines were never relieved by new detachments, like the soldiers, and they endured the entire lifetime of the settlement. Boredom was a major problem.

Not all marines in New Holland had such little to do as their duties depended on their posting. Elsewhere they guarded convicts and were involved with the system of convict transportation. Some were used to hunt down bushrangers, or saw action in the suppression of armed resistance by Indigenous Australians, and they assisted local police to maintain public order. Marines also undertook ceremonial duties such as firing ceremonial artillery salutes, and developed the nation's military defences. They ran quarantine stations and some government houses and manned coastal defences, built fortifications, put out fires, organised executions, provided guards for wrecks and mounted escorts for moving gold from the goldfields. They also fought at Eureka Stockade.

The cannons the marines installed on Melville Island were standard British 9-pounder naval guns with a maximum range of 1550 metres, and an effective range of 830 metres [144]. Also, a 12-pounder gun and four 18-pounder guns, with 'fifty rounds of shot and eight rounds of grape shot' each, were provided for use in close-up warfare. These latter were actually useless, due to a lack of suitable carronade carriages: long-gun carriages, which these carronades did not fit, had been sent by mistake [66].

The plan was that, with the big cannons sited at both the fort

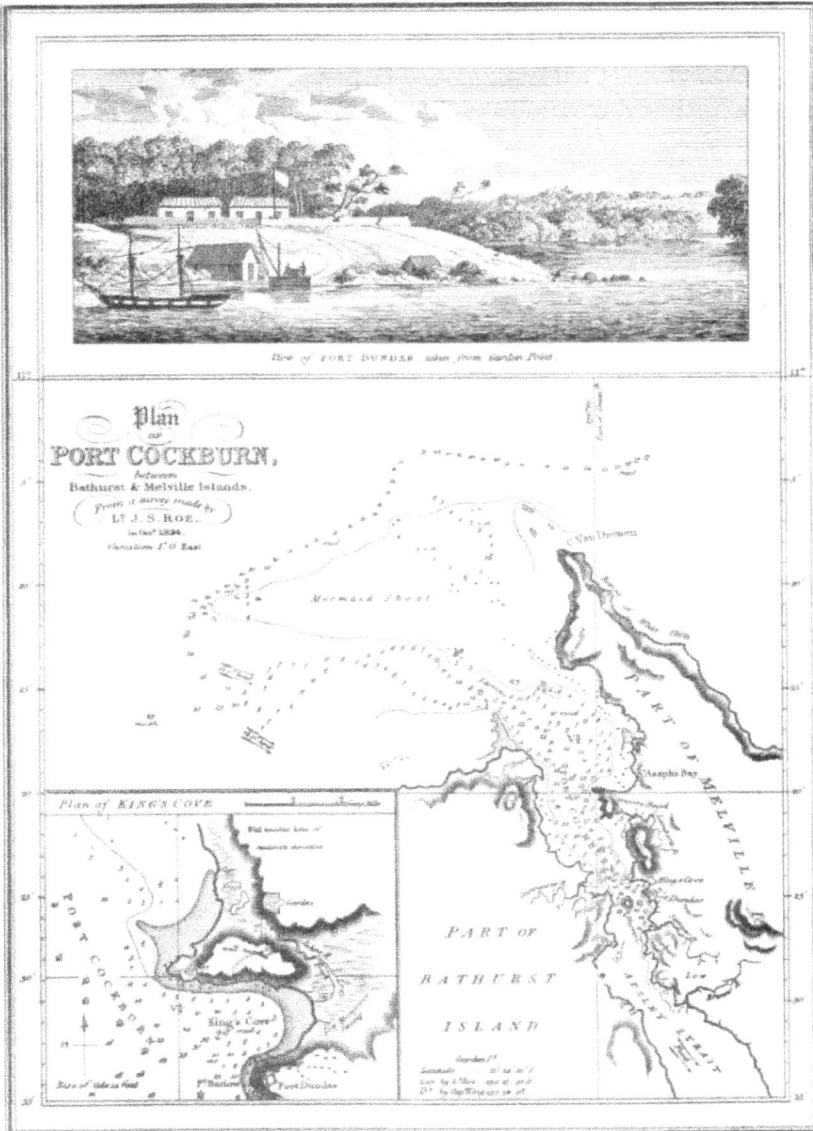

Figure 6 Top: JS Roe's sketch of the fort as seen from Garden Point. This appeared in King's narrative75 in 1827. HMS Lady Nelson is moored in front of the commissariat. The cloud formation depicted is a reliable weather phenomenon these days known as Hector. The cloud formation depicted is a reliable weather phenomenon these days known as Hector. Bottom: A chart of Apsley Strait between Bathurst and Melville islands and Port Cockburn, from a survey made by Lieutenant J.S. Roe in October 1824, with a plan of King Cove inset

25

and on Harris Island in the middle of the strait, the marines could set up a crossfire so that any unwelcome intruders coming towards them would easily be sunk or turned away.

Marines were supposed to be ship-based with time on shore, but the settlement didn't have ship-board accommodation. The men and their families, if they had them, lived in the settlement in huts

They made themselves, probably out of wattle and daub and thatched with grass they had collected from near the fort. On 30 October 1824, a grass-cutting party first experienced the Tiwi resistance to the Britons' arrival. A party of about sixty armed Tiwi surrounded five marines who were collecting grass, and shouted and gestured towards them. They threw a few spears to reinforce their point but wisely stayed back when they saw the marines were armed. However, later a smaller group surrounded Corporal Gwillan and a midshipman from the *Tamar* and an altercation followed which ended with Gwillan firing at one of the Tiwi at close range, killing him. Six months later Gwillan* was speared to death, perhaps in revenge [44].

A number of ordinary sailors also fell under the Commandant's command whilst at the fort. Many of them were only there briefly, and they usually lived aboard their ships when in Port Cockburn. Some, like Captain Samuel Johns† and the entire crew of the *Lady Nelson,* were government employees assigned to the settlement, but the crew of the *Stedcombe* worked for Captain Barns. These crewmen, and many of the other sailors at Fort Dundas, were such transient visitors that most of their names are were not recorded.

The settlement's first medical officer was Charles Turner MD, who signed his letters, 'Assistant Surgeon, Royal Artillery.' Assistant Surgeons were not doctors as we understand the term now, as they had only basic military medical training, more designed to patch

---

* Samuel Gwillan was listed in Turner's *Return of the Sick* several times prior to his death, suffering from ulcers and 'rheumatismus.'

† Captain Johns discovered the permanent fresh water creek that fills the billabong on Garden Point. The creek is still called *Johns River,* and it remains the water source for the Pirlangimpi Community.

up the wounded in battle than heal diseases. Although they were called 'Doctor' by their patients, they titled themselves 'MD' and could not officially be known as doctors until they received a degree. Little is known about the three Fort Dundas doctors; although they were young (the third, Sherwin, was twenty-two years old), with little experience and poor knowledge of tropical medicine.

Charles Turner wrote a letter soon after arriving at Fort Dundas to a man named Wilkinson, who shared it with the East India Trade Committee in London, where it arrived in April 1825. The members of the committee were excited and encouraged by the letter and sent a deputation to RW Horton MP, expressing their hope that Earl Bathurst would soon be encouraging emigrant settlers to Melville Island. It was probably written in November or December 1824, as those months are when the wet season generally arrives.

"We have established ourselves in this part of the world and the island appears to afford the advantages that have induced the Government to send the expedition. The Latitude is 11 degrees 23 minutes south and the Longitude is 130 degrees 27 minutes East of Greenwich. The entrance to Port Cockburn is at the North West extremity about five miles in extent. It affords most excellent Anchorages within pistol shot of the settlement. A stream of fresh water sufficient for any supply runs close to the Fort. The climate is of course very warm but the daily sea breezes render it delightful and the detachment under my care prove it to be healthy, at least for the few weeks that have passed since our arrival. The island is low and very thickly wooded in every part. This is the period that we are expecting the rainy season with the Westerly Monsoon and I suppose that we shall be visited by the Malays in a short period. We are in perfect security and as a depot for the produce of the Archipelago it will answer every purpose. Representations should be made to the Emigrants from China to induce them to settle amongst us. Our communications with Sydney can scarcely be by any other channel

than the Isle de France, at least for some time to come." [138]

Assistant Surgeon Turner completed a two-year posting at the fort and was relieved by John Gold in September 1826. During his time, he had taken part in the establishment of the settlement and the building of the sixteen-bed weatherboard hospital, but he had helplessly watched the health of the population deteriorating. He thought that scurvy resulted from 'privations' arising from 'exhaustion of labour in a tropical environment and exposure to damp during the rainy season.' [138] Unfortunately, he left few records outlining his thoughts and feelings about life there, but he did desperately request to be allowed to 'quit the settlement' after only eight months on the island.

In the British Army, the commissariat was the department that organised the logistics of day-to-day life. It was staffed by uniformed civilians, and by its very nature the commissariat required men of the highest integrity to function properly. At Fort Dundas, the procurement of supplies was a challenging task, but more than twelve months' worth was delivered by the *Countess of Harcourt* in the first days. The main food items in the store included flour, biscuits, salted meat (beef and pork), suet, raisins, peas, oatmeal, rice, and sugar. The settlers could also buy tea, soap, tobacco, gin, and rum. The commissariat was able to substitute fish for meat as part of the rations when it was available. Rations were not allocated equally, as status divided the community. The convicts were the lowest level of the settlement and they were fed the most basic of diets. Raisins, which contain Vitamin C, were probably reserved for the officers, for none of them developed scurvy. Only two marines and two soldiers of the 3rd were listed on Assistant Surgeon Turner's *Return of the Sick* with the disease, so they may also have been issued with them. Without any real understanding of the disease, Turner organised an upgrade of the convicts' diet to include preserved meat and spirits in an attempt to fight scurvy.

Naturally, the commissariat store was one of the very first buildings to be constructed at Fort Dundas, and it was huge, measuring over eighteen metres in length and five metres in width. It was made of heavy timber with a thatched roof and also had a loft, with a high double window for ventilation*. George Miller, the clerk in charge, was able to transfer the goods from the *Countess of Harcourt* for storage in this grand building by early November. It was built near the water's edge, adjacent to the pier, and curiously, in a place which would have made it an easy target for any attacking ships if they ever came. The commissariat building appears in several of the sketches and watercolour paintings from the time, but it is depicted as smaller than it is reputed to have been. It needed to be remodelled after a few months to hold the 'wet provisions.'

George Miller was a 'Treasury Appointment' as Clerk in Charge of the Commissariat. His was a demanding role ensuring correct ordering of supplies and managing the logistics of the settlement. Many of his letters survive, for example this one to Captain Barlow:

"Melville Island
6th March 1826,

Sir,

I have the honor to advise the receipt in Dundas into His Magesty's Magazines of Pickles 3783 pounds Sauce 228 pints Sallid oil 144 pints Mustard 188 pounds
Which I am instructed are at your disposal for the service of the settlement.

I have the honor to be
&c &c &c

---

* A description of the windows appears in a court hearing transcript of the convict John Simpson.

29

George Miller"

Miller had arrived in Sydney in 1822 from Perth in Scotland and showed considerable talents for business and money management. In 1823, he was a clerk in charge of cash payments, but he applied at once when the call for volunteers came for Fort Dundas, hoping for a quick route to promotion. He was appointed from August 1824, and stayed for nearly the entire time the settlement existed, but ill health in 1828 earned him two months leave back in Sydney.

Captain Bremer thought highly of George Miller, and as he left the island, he recorded:

> *"I may here gratify myself at least by bearing witness, through documents of authority, to the value of an old friend in the public service, whose merits—at so great a distance from the seat of authority—were so tardily and scantily acknowledged; and when acknowledged, were so shabbily waived." (Extract from General Order 1827)*

The Asian water buffalo nowadays is a feral species across the Top End of Australia which can cause huge environmental damage. It was first introduced into the country via Fort Dundas, imported from Timor, and Miller himself travelled to Koepang (Kupang) in 1826 to purchase some. He reported to the commandant that buffaloes varied in price according to their size, but that those costing five Spanish dollars in Timor were the right size for shipment on the *Mermaid*, although most of those that eventually arrived on Melville Island cost considerably more than that. In Timor, Miller attempted to establish a regular supply of all provisions to the settlement, but this was a difficult task. He dealt mainly with a secretary of the Dutch government, a Mr Zillman, and from him he bought twenty buffalo, eight of which died on the voyage home. He also bought a supply of twenty pekuls* of Indian corn at one dollar per pekul and

* A pekul weighed 124 lbs or 56.2 kg

paddy (unhusked rice) at two dollars. Husked rice cost five dollars per pekul. But vegetables were few and far between because Timor did not produce enough for export, but there were other exotic goods brought in from Batavia, such as handkerchiefs, iron, gunpowder and fruits that could possibly be traded.

With contacts in place on 22 October 1826, Miller, using Spanish dollars, ordered:

> *"… thirty buffaloes landed at the Settlement in good condition, twenty Spanish dollars each and for twenty five sheep, two and a half dollars and for ten of the larger sheep, four dollars each landed and also in good condition."*

When Fort Dundas was transferred to Raffles Bay, the buffaloes they could catch were taken with them. Any that had escaped revelled in their new environment and their descendants are still hunted today by the Tiwi. Ironically, it was buffalo hunting that brought the next Europeans to the Tiwi Islands, nearly seventy years later.

Miller went to Sydney for his sick leave in 1828, but never returned to Fort Dundas as it was shut down soon after. Campbell mentioned him in his journal when writing about health and the effects of the tropical climate, stating that Miller 'suffered much from the climate' and 'remained in a very debilitated state for a year and more after leaving the island.' From Sydney, Miller took up a position of management in the commissariat in Port Macquarie. There was also a George Miller who was the Director of the Sydney Banking Company in the 1840s who could have been him; although it was a common name.

One trade Miller was not interested in was that of slavery. Briefly banned by Raffles during his years in charge of the East Indies during the Napoleonic Wars, slavery had returned with the Dutch, and the huge slave market in Batavia was once again trading. The Dutch Resident in Timor told Miller that an English vessel (under Dutch colours) had landed at Flores and demanded the Rajah there sell them a full cargo of slaves in the 'service of the Dutch Government.' When the Rajah hesitated, the slavers seized him and threatened to carry him off to Batavia for punishment if the order was not fulfilled. The Rajah had come in Koepang to complain to the Resident of his treatment only weeks before Miller's visit.

The clerks and storemen of the commissariat kept stock of everything and ordered what was needed. Because transport was so slow, the commissariat officers were required to meticulously plan for produce and equipment months ahead of when it would be needed. The Melville Island commissariat was the only source of material goods for purchase anywhere on the north coast of the continent.

Besides Miller, several other men were fully employed in the commissariat: Joseph Radford ran the stores on a daily timetable, opening about seven in the morning and closing about four in the afternoon. Opening hours meant that soldiers, marines and convicts would be issued with equipment, food or clothing as was permitted. There was also a daily ration of alcohol and Commissariat Officer William Ladbrook was the 'proper person employed for the purpose' of issuing it. He would ring a bell at eleven in the morning and issue pints of rum to the men until noon, drawing the pints from a 'scuttled butt' and mixing it with a quart of water for each man over twenty years old who wanted it. Sometimes there were special occasions when Radford would open the store at different times, but usually the rules were strictly followed. Radford served at Fort Dundas for its entire existence, and moved to Fort Wellington at Raffles Bay when Fort Dundas closed down. Sadly, he died there on 24 July 1828, and he is now remembered in the name of Radford Road in Howard Springs, near Darwin. Other commissariat storekeepers, clerks and issuers who served at Fort Dundas include George Talmash* who arrived with the first ships

---

* Ennis (1825) mentions a Mr Tamash as being a storeman who travelled and stayed several years. When he left the island is unknown, but by 1828 he had been replaced by John Henry Green

George Miller had an assigned convict servant named William Bullock, who was a fair headed, freckle-faced boy†. Miller's assistant clerk, William Raymond, who was at the Fort in the latter days of Fort Dundas, possibly arriving with Captain Hartley, also had a convict assigned to him as his servant, named Patrick Healy‡. Bullock and Healy found themselves travelling to Melville Island when their employer was posted there, and it seems likely that they did not 'volunteer' in the normal sense of the word, but took a posting to Fort Dundas as part of their duties to those to whom they were assigned.

There may have been other settlers for whom the records are lost. Some of the marines and soldiers had their wives and children with them on their postings, but we mostly do not know who they were or how many. Campbell said six women were at the settlement when he arrived, but not all of their names appear in the records. We only hear of Mary Tobin, for example, because she had a baby. Another woman, named Sarah Fearly, collected Assistant Surgeon Gold's personal items together after his death and made a list of his jewellery, noting that some items were brought from England and that *she* had bought others in Sydney [107]. Unfortunately, there is no

---

with Barlow on the *Tamar* to Melville Island[52], Morris[91] and *The Monthly Magazine*[90] (1824) called him Talmash and others, like Street[132] called him George Tollemache.

† Bullock had stolen a trunk full of clothing and had been given a seven-year sentence. He arrived with Miller in 1824 and he stayed there with him for four years until July 1828. It is likely that Bullock accompanied Miller when he returned to Sydney on his sick leave as a ticket-of-leave man. He was freed in 1829, and he married Ann Walker. Together they made their home in Parramatta.

‡ Healy was a young, ruddy, freckle-faced Irishmen from Cork, sentenced for stealing money and transported for seven years in 1826. He was a literate 'indoor servant and groom,' and when he arrived in Sydney, he was assigned to Mr Raymond. He served at the fort until the last few months of the settlement when he returned with Raymond to Sydney in the *Lucy Ann* in November 1828.

other information about who she was, where she came from, or why she was there, but because convict records were relatively well kept, it seems unlikely she was a convict. Was she Gold's wife?

Barlow employed the three volunteers, Potter, Feathers, and Chapman who answered Bremer's advertisement in Sydney to use their trades in the construction of the settlement. All three were ex-convicts, and they survived their time at the fort, but little is known about their lives there. They all returned to Sydney after a few years and then faded into history. The first, William Potter, was a nail maker and blacksmith in Sydney. He had been transported to New Holland in 1815 and had worked whilst still a convict as a servant in Parramatta. He earned a ticket-of-leave by 1821 and his freedom at the end of his sentence. For a while, he was a constable, but was later dismissed for gross misconduct. He signed up to go to Fort Dundas willingly, but what reason he had to do so remains unknown—perhaps he just needed a job. The copper nails found at the fort by archaeologists may well have been made by him. On one list he is identified as a 'nail maker and *potter,*' but it is possible there was some confusion about his name.

The second volunteer was Henry Feathers who had been indicted as an eighteen-year-old lad with three others for picking a five-shilling yellow handkerchief from an unknown gentleman's pocket. The boys had worked together as a gang, all the time being closely watched by the constable who arrested them. Feathers was sentenced to transportation for life, and he arrived in Sydney in 1818. He was a brick maker and he volunteered to join the settlement, even though he had already earned himself a ticket-of-leave before 1823. Then twenty-three-years old, perhaps he was seeking adventure. He returned to Sydney on the *Isabella* in 1826 and thereafter disappears from the records.

The third free settler was Edward Chapman. He had arrived in Australia as a convict in 1816 and had served his full sentence, earning his Certificate of Freedom in July 1824. In August, the Acting Engineer of the Colony of New South Wales, Major John

34

Ovens, offered him a job. Their agreement was that Chapman would go to Fort Dundas as a sawyer and work for six months for the Government on a half-time basis and be allowed after that to return to Sydney. The government provided him with free passage and provisions, but were tardy in shipping him home. In the end it was not until 10 October 1826, more than two years later, before Chapman would return on the *Isabella*.

Another free settler was Captain William Barns, the trader who first promoted the idea of a settlement to Earl Bathurst in London. He arrived in Fort Dundas in February 1825. He had asked for an official position in the settlement but Bathurst had refused him [73]. Nevertheless, he continued to throw his full support behind the new settlement and, as he now skippered the schooner *Stedcombe* (which was owned by members of the East India Trade Committee), he was there to begin a business. Barlow allowed Barns some land near the waterfront to build a storehouse and two acres near the gardens to grow wheat. He was plainly instructed that the waterfront land was just on loan, in case Barlow's successor thought of a better use for it by the government. This was good planning because when Commandant Campbell took over from Barlow, he was horrified that Barns had 'occupied the very best place upon which a Wharf and Store House could be built in the Neighbourhood of the cove', and he declared to the Colonial Secretary that Barns would certainly be dispossessed as soon as the Government required the land [36].

As it happened, Barns and the *Stedcombe* had arrived just in time—scurvy had appeared and some of the settlers were sickening quickly, provisions were low and their agricultural pursuits were so far unsuccessful. The *Lady Nelson* had sailed just four days earlier for supplies, and as a backup, the *Stedcombe* was immediately chartered to purchase more buffalo and vegetables from the Indies. Commandant Barlow agreed to pay twenty-five Spanish dollars per buffalo if they weighed more than 250 pounds.

Barns stayed behind in the fort to begin work on his land, and he

35

sent his first mate, Mr Bastell, to skipper the schooner for its potentially short trip for victuals. How often Barns must have wondered at his fate, for the *Stedcombe* never returned. Later it was learned that pirates off Timor Laut had captured her and all the crew had been killed, apart from the two cabin boys (see Chapter 9). Barns was then stranded on the island until he could get a passage south. During this time, he continually exasperated Captain Barlow with his 'high-handed' manner. He ignored Barlow's requests to pay his convict workers with 'tobacco or slops' instead of liquor and the commandant found this to be a tremendous annoyance [29]. Barlow tried his best to cope with Barns, despite, he said, being 'forced to listen' to his 'many fine speeches.' Fort Dundas was, after all, a very small community. Later, back in Sydney, Governor Darling agreed with Barlow's opinion and described Barns as 'an unprincipled adventurer totally unworthy of notice' whose 'object appears to be purely speculative'.

Morale sunk as several of the men were speared by local Tiwi warriors, and the settlers became virtually besieged within the fort, unable to leave it unless in armed groups. Nevertheless, in August 1825, Barlow was inexplicably upbeat. He wrote that scurvy was under control and a regular supply of cattle was about to arrive, fresh from Sydney. His cheerful report was in stark contrast to other letters coming from the settlement, specifically from Captain Barns, originally the most optimistic of them all. Barns became spiteful and bitter after he was stranded on the island by the loss of the *Stedcombe*. He wrote to Mr Begbie of the East India Trade Committee that the settlement was 'in great distress for want of provisions' without even a boat for fishing. Fort Dundas was a 'miserable hole', he said, and was:

> "...*too far west, and off the trepang grounds altogether, and it is my firm opinion that if we stay here until the day of resurrection it will be a place of no consequence in the commercial world.*" [12]

Over the next year, Commandant Barlow requested a transfer and he was eventually relieved. He wasn't the only one who wanted to leave. His second in command, Lieutenant Richard Everard wrote to his sister on 24 September 1826 describing Melville Island as a 'hell upon Earth.'

> "I have at length to announce to you, my dearest Fanny, the joyful news of a vessel having arrived here… from Sydney to take us down there once more, and to be relieved from this delectable place, which I can assure you I shall leave with a very light heart, and that I hailed the arrival of the relief with cheers, nine times nine. There is neither honour nor glory to be obtained by remaining here, save that of being commandant…
>
> With regard to the HMS Lady Nelson, it was only in April 1825 that we were enabled to get any provisions, as I mentioned to you in my last we feared that the Colonial brig that was sent to Tymor (sic) for stock had been cut off by the Malay pirates, and we have every reason now to suppose that she has been, as we never had had any account of her since.
>
> One cannot venture far out into the bush to shoot by way of recreation (and lately not out of sight of the settlement) with safety, for fear of being surprised by the natives, they having speared not fewer than nine men, one of whom died of his wounds and another lost the sight of an eye. The clearing gangs are obliged to go out to work with armed firelocks" [55]

The 3rd Regiment regrouped in Sydney in 1827. Forty-seven of them transferred to other regiments or the Mounted Police, so they could stay in New South Wales. The rest were moved to a new posting in Calcutta, in December. Barlow was then probably one of the two hundred officers and men of the 3rd who died within a few weeks of arrival in Calcutta during an epidemic of cholera, as he was not listed among those who returned to England [117, 22]. He is remembered in the name of Barlow Place in The Narrows, a suburb of Darwin, and, according to *The*

Queenslander in 1937, as a 'pioneer of the Buffalo Industry,' as it was he, with Commissariat Officer Miller, who brought in the first Asian water buffalo. Tom Cole praised the captain in his book *The Buffalo Hunters* and described how Barlow ordered fifteen buffalo from a French trader named Monsieur Charles Bechard in Timor after the loss of the *Lady Nelson* and *Stedcombe*, but only had three delivered alive. 'A lesser man would be forgiven for abandoning the undertaking,' wrote Cole, but Barlow went on to arrange the delivery of two hundred buffalo per year. Over the next three years it's likely that about two hundred buffalo in total ever arrived at Fort Dundas, transported in the brigs *Ann* and *Marcus*. It was enough. Despite many of them being used for food, those that escaped or were released had thousands of descendants within seventy years, which roamed free across Melville Island and the Top End of Australia.

5

CAMPBELL

Major John Campbell and his men from the 57th Regiment arrived in Port Cockburn on the *HMS Isabella* on 19 September 1826, and took over from the exhausted Barlow and the 'Buffs.' It was almost exactly two years after the settlement was first carved out of the bush. Campbell reported that:

> *"Of land cleared of timber there were fifty-two acres, three of them cultivated; and ninety-five acres on which the timber was fenced, but not cleared off. The buildings consisted of three wooden houses for officers, one for soldiers, one for a hospital, two store-houses, thirteen huts for the prisoners, and seven for the Royal Marines. The huts were in general miserable hovels, constructed hastily and irregularly."* [33]

The colonial cutter *HMS Mermaid* arrived the day after the *Isabella* under the command of Captain Samuel Dowsett[51]. The *Mermaid* was the replacement, at long last, of the lost *Lady Nelson,* and she was fresh from Timor with a cargo of buffalo. She also carried confirmation that the schooner *Stedcombe* had been taken by Malay pirates the year before.

Like Barlow, Campbell's initial impression and reports were positive, despite his consternation that the settlement hadn't advanced as far as he had expected over its first two years. However, over time he became less and less happy in his posting. Campbell is better known than Barlow and his successor Hartley, because he wrote a lengthy paper about Melville Island for the Royal Geographical Society in 1834. He wrote elegantly on a wide range of topics, but seven years earlier, at the end of two years of privations and tremendous strain, he had seen little to write positively about. Having arrived excited and optimistic, within a few months, he seemed burned out and sick of the whole business. He had had a phenomenal workload in managing the settlement and having to deal with surly, resistant convicts and soldiers alike, and it had worn him down. On 11 November 1827, in a letter to the Colonial Secretary, he begged:

"I have had a complete surfeit of this island and sincerely hope His Excellency will order me to be immediately relieved."

The 57th Regiment of Foot, also called the West Middlesex Regiment of Foot, dates back to an amalgamation of several regiments in 1756. The regiment was given their nickname *the Die-Hards* after fighting with distinction in the Battle of Albuera in 1811. This was the bloodiest battle of the Peninsular War, when 422 out of the 570 men in the ranks and twenty out of the thirty officers were killed with their commanding officer, mortally wounded himself, apparently shouting:

"Die hard the 57th, die hard!"

The 57th Regiment had shipped out to Australia in a number of convict transports between October 1824 and December 1825. Major Campbell was with the detachment that left on 4 November 1824 and Lieutenant John Ovens, who was to become his second in command
40

at Fort Dundas, the next May. Like the Buffs before them, in Sydney the 57th were split up and spread out across the colonies. Detachments were sent to Norfolk Island, Melville Island, Van Diemen's Land, and Moreton Bay; although their headquarters always remained in Sydney under the command of Lieutenant Colonel Shadforth.

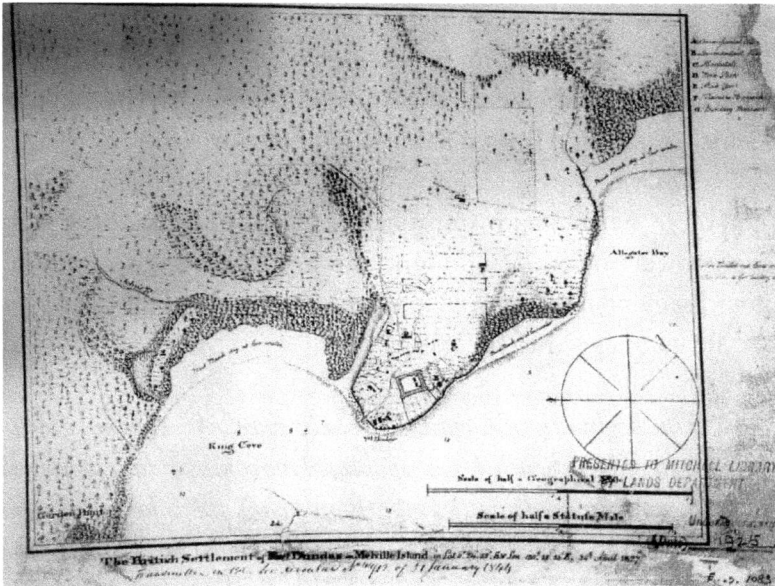

Figure 7 Map of Fort Dundas drawn by Major Campbell in 1827. The fort is shown as larger than is really was. The gardens of Garden Point are on the lower left. Footpaths are shown which led to the gardens and to the Johns River water source.

When the forty-three men of the 57th arrived to relieve the remains of the detachment from the 3rd Regiment, they would have been keen to hear the stories from the old hands about the previous two years. Unlike the convicts, soldiers did not volunteer for such remote duties; they went where the regiment sent them. What the soldiers or convicts thought was never written down or recorded in any way, so their thoughts are lost forever; although, as Powell says:

> ..." *the petty quarrels and tensions of a bored and insecure garrison bore heavily on the Commandant's nerves, and ... their feelings*

41

came out in drunkenness, indiscipline, and in nearly every prisoner leaving the settlement by the first vessel after his sentence expired."[107]

Five soldiers of the 57th lost their lives on Melville Island. At least three died of a fever in the first few weeks of 1827. Another, Corporal Patrick Brown, died of food poisoning. In his curiosity to try a 'resource other than the commissariat,' Brown had eaten the castor oil plant *Ricinus communis,* which grew in the settlement gardens as a purgative medicine. The plant's high level of ricin makes it extremely toxic, and Brown paid the ultimate price for his foraging (Calley 2000).

In 1834, when Major Campbell read his memoir to the Royal Geographical Society of London, he was not adverse to some self-aggrandisement and appeared to forget the despair of his last reports when he had begged to be relieved.

> *"At the beginning of August, 1826, His Excellency General Darling, Governor of New South Wales, appointed me commandant of Melville Island, and directed me to embark on board the colonial schooner Isabella, with a detachment of troops, some convicts, and various stores, as well as livestock, and to proceed with all despatch through Torres Strait to relieve Captain Barlow and his detachment. On August 19th we left Port Jackson, and reached Melville Island on September 19th. The officers and men who had formed the settlement, and had been there about two years, were rejoiced to find that relief had arrived for them. They gave us a discouraging account of the oppressiveness of the climate, the scarcity of vegetables, the deficiency of meat, the almost impossibility of procuring fish, the dreariness of the situation (having only been visited by the two small colonial vessels already mentioned, by a man-of-war's boat, which came in for a few hours whilst the man-of-war, the 'Slaney' remained outside, eighteen miles off; and I believe that H.M.S. 'Lome' had touched there), the hostility of the natives—all this conveyed a gloomy picture of the settlement.*

I was, however, fortunately not of a temperament to be cast down by these accounts; but on the contrary rejoiced that I had been placed in so novel and interesting a situation, and looked forward with a pleasing anticipation that patience, exertion, and industry would soon bring the settlement to answer the intentions of Government in having formed it." [33]

In 1827, Campbell cancelled permission for June Richardson, the gardener's wife and a free woman, to travel to Sydney for health reasons because of her husband's behaviour, and Street was clearly not impressed by him:

"This quite unwarranted and unreasonable punishment of a free woman because of the behaviour of her convict husband paved the way for her early death. It also left us a clear picture of a petty tyrant whose perception was so limited that he was unable to… enable his tiny garrison to successfully occupy this isolated defensive position." [132]

In 1827, Campbell was pleased to greet Lieutenant William Hicks who arrived in command of the Government vessel, the *Mary Elizabeth,* which was to be stationed at Melville Island for trading runs to Timor, relieving the Mermaid. Hicks was a naval officer who made a longer lasting impression on the community than most. He had been a seventeen-year-old midshipman at the Battle of Trafalgar* and first arrived in Sydney as an officer on a convict ship transporting women in 1818. He liked New Holland and requested permission to stay, but he'd been caught in compromising situations with some of the women convicts and was denied permission as punishment. He returned four years later and managed to get a land grant in the

---

* Hicks' naval uniform from the Battle of Trafalgar survives and is held in the National Maritime Museum in London. It is in excellent condition and the only known uniform from that battle.

Hunter River Region of over a thousand acres. He also found a bride, and on 18 November 1823, he married Sophie Hickey, a daughter of John Hickey of Bent Street, Sydney. Sophie was a free woman who had arrived in 1818 with her mother, brothers, and sisters.

Hicks wasn't a success at farming, and following an attack by bushrangers, he left the land to return to the sea, gratefully accepting his first command. *HMS Mary Elizabeth* carried a number of volunteer convicts and some soldiers from the 39th Regiment of Foot who were dropped off at Fort Wellington before moving the ship on to Melville Island (see Appendix 5). Sophie, pregnant with their second child, was also on board with their two-year-old son, William. The family settled into life at Fort Dundas as best they could, and Sophie prepared for the new baby. Sadly, when she went into labour on 2 November 1827 things did not go well and both Sophie, and the baby girl died. Sophie may be the first European woman settler to die in northern Australia, and her grave is still visible at the site of Fort Dundas. Next to it stands the memorial plaque remembering all thirty-three of the settlers who died there. The unnamed baby is not listed.

In 1828, the Hobart Town Courier reported the death of Sophie and their *two* children at Melville Island. This was incorrect because Hicks later applied to go to Timor to pick up the younger William who was staying there. Hicks and his son arrived back in Sydney on the *Mary Elizabeth* in August 1828. He continued to command the *Mary Elizabeth,* making numerous voyages to Port Macquarie and Moreton Bay, and at least one to the Isle de France.

For millennia, all the babies born in Northern Australia were children of the Aboriginal tribes who lived there. If the Macassan visitors included pregnant women on the annual trepang fishing journeys to Australia, then there may have been Australian born Asians, but European births in northern Australia before 1827 are unlikely. Sophie Hicks wasn't the first settler to have a baby in the fort. The first was Elizabeth Melville Richardson, daughter of June and John Richardson the gardener (see Chapter 7), born on 27

March 1827. Elizabeth was a strong baby and she thrived, despite her mother's ailing health. June died when Elizabeth was three years old, and she was raised by John through the 1830s. She moved to Victoria during the gold rush years and married, firstly James Bisgrove and later Francis Feltis. She had three daughters with Feltis (Jane, Mary, and Francis) and raised them in Victoria. Elizabeth died in Victoria in 1910 at the age of eighty-three years and has numerous descendants still living there, many of whom are proud that their ancestor was the first European born in North Australia.

The second child was Ellen Sadleir, the daughter of Private William Sadleir of the 57th Regiment of Foot and Mary Tobin. She was born during 1828. Ellen was Mary's eighth child, but their first six children had all died in infancy (William and Mary had sixteen children, five of whom survived). Ellen's older brother James had arrived with their parents at the fort in early 1828 as a robust three-year-old, and both he and Ellen turned out to be healthy and strong children. Sadlier may have left the 57th Regiment after his Fort Dundas posting, as the family stayed in New South Wales during the 1830s. Ellen died in Young, New South Wales, in 1913, during her eighty-sixth year.

Another woman living in the settlement was a free settler named Katherine Tiernam (aka Tierney). She had followed her husband Patrick, a shoemaker, all the way from Liverpool in England to New South Wales after he had been sentenced to seven years for stealing seven shillings and sixpence. Katherine arrived in Sydney in April 1824, with their daughter Elizabeth, and then also travelled to Melville Island with Patrick and the other convicts on the *Countess of Harcourt*. Unfortunately, Patrick died of scurvy at the settlement sixteen months later. Widowed, Katherine remained on the island with her daughter, and eventually married another convict named William Nixon. Nixon was a lifer, transported for highway robbery of £38 and a watch. His trade was in cotton dyeing and spinning, plus he was a wheelwright. They were married on 12 November 1826, by Assistant Surgeon John

Gold JP, in the first European wedding performed in North Australia, witnessed by John Richardson—the gardener—and his wife June.

When Katherine became pregnant with William's baby, she and Elizabeth returned to Sydney to have the child, Sarah Ann, in September 1827, and she then petitioned for her husband to be allowed to join her in Sydney. When this was refused, she continued to display extraordinary loyalty and returned to Melville Island with the children to be with her husband. The family remained there until nearly the end of the settlement when, in September 1828, they were all returned to Sydney on the *Governor Phillip*. They lived on Kent Street, and Katherine had two more daughters, Mary Ann and Louisa, but Katherine died in 1834, aged forty-one years. Nixon, whose own brand of loyalty seems to have not measured up to Katherine's, couldn't cope with four daughters, and he put them in the Female Orphan School to be raised on charity. He lived the rest of his life on Kent Street, dying alone in 1862, aged fifty-eight years.

The medical officer who cared for these women and delivered June's baby, was John Gold MD. Gold arrived with Campbell on the *Isabella*, which had left Sydney in September 1826 with his convict servant, William Henrys*. Gold wasn't a military man as none could be found to replace Turner. He was, therefore, offered a special salary, which was recorded as a guinea a day *[111]*. Gold may have been a good doctor, but he also seemed to have had no more idea about the causes of scurvy than did Major Campbell, and men continued to die needlessly as they had for centuries during the 'Age of Sail.'

A letter from Assistant Surgeon Gold to his mother survives† in which he describes his newfound situation and is, in hindsight, prophetic:

> *"...this is so unfrequented a part of the world that it is a matter*
> *of difficult accomplishment to get away even if I should feel desirous*

---

* William Henrys was a young carpenter from Chelsea whose crime had been the theft of some leather from a house.

† This letter is in private hands, and it sold at auction in 2008 for $43,000.

*to do so...the climate is favourable to the production of disease... The
hospital is a small but comfortable building...and it is generally full.
The men have lately suffered from scurvy, malignant fever, and other
endemick diseases of a dangerous character. Besides these evils, we are
subject to another nearly as formidable. Scarcely a week elapses but
our men are endangered by visits of the Aborigines who are very wild
and hostile in spite of all the kindness we can possibly show them..."""*

Gold is most remembered for his violent death from the very Aborigines
he told his mother about. On 2 November 1827, he and John Green, a
storekeeper, had attended Sophie Hicks' funeral and later were outside
the settlement, walking towards the gardens, when they met a party of
Tiwi. He may have been there against "orders," but he was a civilian
and he behaved as one. Campbell was away at Fort Wellington at the
time, and the officer in charge of the settlement was Lieutenant Bate,
whose authority Gold did not recognise at all. What went on between
the two Englishmen and the Tiwi is not known, but Gold and Green
were speared to death. There were no witnesses and the settlers had to
send out search parties for them after they were noticed missing. Green's
body was found fairly quickly. As Hicks recorded later, at 6:15pm:

*"... the alarm was given that the natives had surrounded Mr. Green
and Dr Gold who had walked towards the path; shortly afterwards
the body of Mr. Green was found and brought dead into the fort, and
Lieutenant Bates and myself attentively examined it, and found the
following wounds: Mr. Green had received in all 17 wounds from
spears - three were in his throat, one through his arm, ten in front
of his body, and one in his back; he had also two severe cuts on the
head, one was about six inches long, the lips above two inches deep,
the skull laid open, so that the brains could be distinctly seen."* [133]

Gold's body was discovered by a twenty-three-year-old convict
tailor, Thomas Swan, the next morning. Swan carried a musket,

and he fired a shot to signal to the community. The body must have been a gruesome sight as Gold had been killed in a frenzy of spear stabbing.

> *"Nov. 3, AM 7 the body of Mr. Gold brought into the fort by the party who had been sent in search of it, and had the following wounds in it as were found by myself and Lieut. Bates. On the body 31 spear wounds, in seven of which the heads were still sticking, several of the spears had gone through the body and head, and one appeared to have penetrated the bowels, several wounds were in his legs, and from every circumstance I should fear he had died very hard."[133]*

Gold's servant, William Henrys, found himself without a job after Gold was killed. Unusually, although he had served two years at the Fort, he was transferred to Raffles Bay when Fort Dundas was abandoned, and he didn't receive a ticket-of-leave until February 1832. It's possible that, as the servant of a Gentleman, Henrys didn't get treated like most others by the Commandants, and the normal reward for his 'volunteering' was overlooked.

Campbell's reports guided the government in their decision-making about the remote fort. It had been clear for several years that it was poorly positioned to be a trading port, but there were other obstacles to its success. In 1834, he informed the Royal Geographical Society that:

> *"Towards the end of 1827 I had sufficient experience to form a more correct opinion of the advantages and disadvantages of Melville Island, and I represented to his Excellency the Governor of New South Wales, the disadvantages under which it laboured, and which appeared to me to counterbalance any argument that could possibly be offered in its favour.*
>
> *Some of the objections were as follows:—'The approach to Apsley Strait was greatly obstructed by shoals; it was out of any direct line of*

trade; the soil near the settlement was generally light and difficult to bring into cultivation; the climate was extremely debilitating, although not decidedly very unhealthy; and the constitutions of Europeans suffered much from its effects.' In the course of twelve months nearly every individual belonging to the establishment had been in hospital, and some of them three or four times. These circumstances, combined with several obstacles, were so much at variance with the prosperity of a young settlement, and had for three years operated so against it, that I felt convinced there was no chance of opening a commercial intercourse between Melville Island and the Indian Archipelago. Thus the main object of the Government in forming an establishment with the view of extending our commerce by introducing European goods throughout the Indian Islands was completely frustrated. From an impression that Melville Island would be abandoned, I directed my attentions more to the east, to that part of the coast of New Holland to which the Malay fishing-prahus resorted every year. I visited Cobourg Peninsula and surveyed Port Essington, which I found to possess many advantages over Port Cockburn." [33]

Victoria Settlement in Port Essington was founded in 1838. Campbell's comments on its suitability may have played a part in the decision:

"The climate of the Cobourg Peninsula must be similar to that of Melville Island. I took a great deal of exercise there, during all hours of the day, as did the thirty persons with me, and none of us experienced even a head-ache. Port Essington being more open to sea breezes, and much freer from mangroves and mud-banks than Apsley Strait, the air must consequently be more pure. I found the temperature the same as at Fort Dundas, but the air is less debilitating along the coast of the Cobourg Peninsula, thereby rendering the human frame less susceptible to disease. In such a situation as Port Essington the mind is also more pleasingly exercised than in Apsley Strait, which I consider another great auxiliary to health." [33]

49

Even as Campbell was relieved, the government wheels were already turning. The settlement was not a success and would not last much longer, and the new commandant, Captain Hartley, certainly wasn't of a mind to support its continuance. Melville Island was the last place he wanted to be.

6

HARTLEY

Captain Humphrey Hartley did not want to go to Melville Island. He was a young and ambitious man who was looking for promotion and managing a remote settlement in such a distant place did not fit in with his life plan at all. According to Captain Laws, Hartley told him he even considered giving up his commission instead of accepting the posting [79]. His lack of interest is more demonstrated by the fact that, once he had arrived, he never ventured more than half a mile from the settlement.

Hartley had shipped out to Sydney with the 57th Regiment some eight months before Major Campbell in March 1825, so he had lived in the colony for nearly three years before he was sent to the fort, in the last week of April 1828. On his way to Melville Island, he spent a few days at the struggling new settlement of Fort Wellington in Raffles Bay. He left depressed at the conditions he observed. Whilst there, he collected thirteen of the sickest convicts and sent them back to Sydney when his transportation, *HMS Sir Phillip Dundas,* returned. He wrote of them in his first report to Colonial Secretary McLeay, two weeks later:

> *"The worn out and emaciated condition of the sick at Raffles Bay and the undue proportion, which their numbers bore to the numerical strength of the population of that settlement, coupled with the generally sickly complexion and attenuated appearance of nearly all afforded a melancholy evidence of the malignant effects of the climate with which they had been contending and which with the accumulated local disadvantages Raffles Bay labours under, appear to render it not only ineligible as a Settlement but moreover unfit for the presence of civilised man."* [67]

Hartley was relieved and perhaps pleasantly surprised by Fort Dundas when he stepped ashore. Only two men were in hospital because of, he said in flattery of a senior officer, 'Major Campbell's zealous and well directed exertions.' Plus, they had plenty of buffalo, and the long dry season lay ahead, so he felt sure those who were developing scurvy would soon pull out of it. Clearly, he was no more aware of the cause of this disease than his predecessors.

In the rest of his report to McLeay, Hartley didn't hold back. On agricultural prospects, he described the soil as 'dry hungry sand' unlikely to ever yield a return; he said he had talked with trepang fishermen near Raffles Bay, who had told him Melville Island was out of their way and they would never call in there. He warned about the danger of the approach to the Apsley Strait, saying that a complex system of navigation buoys was necessary to make it safe. He whinged about the lack of a clerk, the high workload, the 'extreme want of an active, steady and intelligent overseer,' and delays in paying salaries. He complained of the high mortality among the stock he had shipped in the *Sir Phillip Dundas* (they had lost four cows, thirteen sheep, and a bull), and said he had to retain Joseph Van Hammett, a Dutch convict, as a stock-keeper, despite the fact he had been destined to work at Fort Wellington*.

---

* Vanhammett later escaped British custody in 1829 from Fort Wellington, probably by boat.

Hartley was plagued with personal ill-health for most of the time he spent at Fort Dundas, and he seems to have been bed-ridden often. In one miserable comment he said the settlement would prove "…an infirmary for one portion of its population, a cemetery for the other." [67]

The man who cared for him during his illnesses was the third Fort Dundas doctor, William Sherwin MD, who had been in private practice in Sydney but had been convinced, perhaps by the guinea per day salary, to journey north to replace Assistant Surgeon Gold after his violent death. Born in Parramatta in 1804, he was the first Australian to complete his medical studies, albeit in England, graduating with a certificate from the Royal College of Surgeons in 1826. Unfortunately, like all in his profession in those time, Sherwin had little idea of the cause of some of his patients' maladies. His studies in England had taught him little about tropical diseases. His biggest influence was organising the return to Sydney of a number of convicts he worried were too sick to last another wet season, thus saving their lives.

Sherwin returned to Sydney when the Fort closed in 1829 and opened a new private practice in Parramatta. He also farmed cattle and sheep there. One day in 1831, travelling along Windsor Road, Sherwin was held up by a bushranger named McNamara. The bushranger stole his gold watch and any cash he had on him. He later had the watch returned, as a convict named Samuel Horne captured the bushranger. As a reward Horne was pardoned and given a grant of land in an area now named after him: *Hornsby*.

After a few years, Sherwin moved to Sydney and opened a practice on Pitt Street. He returned to England to earn his degree in 1860, from which he could officially be titled 'Doctor.' Back in Australia by 1863, he started lecturing in homeopathies, and today's homeopathic associations consider him the first practitioner of homeopathy in Australia [7].

At Fort Dundas, Hartley and Sherwin were aware of the low morale among the troops and convicts. Complaints and grumblings were heard every day and in June 1828, Hartley wrote:

"... a deep rooted discontent of that portion of the prisoners who bear tickets-of-leave... sullen, dejected, dissatisfied...those who have been longest on the island appear to be most deeply tainted with discontent; they are perpetually indulging in the language of complaint and are constantly alluding to promises made, pledges given, and hopes excited on their originally volunteering to embark for this settlement; and they then point to their present situation and future expectations, and ask whether the former is not of great privation and suffering and the latter clouded with dismal despondency... the health of many of those who have been long upon the island appears to have suffered from the effects of the climate." [67]

With Hartley's report following Campbell's miserable outpourings, the future of the settlement was sealed. Already, on 31 May 1828, the order had been given by Sir George Murray to abandon Fort Dundas and to transfer what could be moved to Fort Wellington. When the orders eventually arrived, Hartley must have been ecstatic, but it still took several months to pack up the livestock, stores and anything useful and ship them to the new fort. The move was completed by 14 February 1829, and Hartley and the last of the convicts, marines, and soldiers sailed away on the *Amity*, leaving Melville Island to the people who had been there for millennia.

Hartley's influence continued, partly because of the length of time it took letters to travel the world. Sir George Murray wrote to Governor Darling on 1 November 1828, but the Governor did not acknowledge the letter until 15 May 1829, when he closed down Fort Wellington as well:

"...the Settlements have proved unhealthy, difficulty is found in supplying them with provisions, and much annoyance is experienced from the Natives. These objections are very serious, and I do not think that there is, on the other side, any prospect of advantage sufficiently strong to warrant a continuance of the Expense and risk of loss of life, by which the Settlements which have been established

at Melville Island and Raffles Bay must be maintained. You will, therefore, upon the receipt of this dispatch, proceed to withdraw the Troops and Convicts who have been stationed there." [99]

Hartley's career was back on track and he went on to other roles in the Regiment. On 12 April 1831, he purchased a promotion, and as a new Lieutenant Colonel, he re-joined the Regiment in Bangalore, India, and took command of the corps there in September 1832. He still suffered health issues, and within a year was back in England on two years sick leave. Hartley's major achievement, of benefit to the entire British army, had its genesis in Fort Dundas. Getting his soldiers paid correctly and on time there was next to impossible because only War Ships were allowed to carry cash, and none ever came the way of the fort. So while he was posted in India, Hartley solved the problem by establishing a Regimental Savings Bank which was:

"An institution equally calculated to fortify discipline, improve morals, and diminish crime, and which in the period of very few months from its introduction produced very important results." [139]

7

THE CONVICTS

Forty-four or forty-five convicts arrived with Bremer in the first days of Fort Dundas, seventeen others followed on the *Sir Phillip Dundas* in 1825, and more came on the *Mermaid*, the *Amity,* and others in subsequent years. In total more than ninety convicts are listed as 'mechanics' (tradesmen), serving their time during the fort's existence, and possibly as many as ninety-eight could claim to have served there, including two women [132]. The exact numbers are confused by time and lost records, and no clarity regarding how many convict servants accompanied the officers. The skills the convicts brought were essential to the establishment of the settlement.

Many were awarded the ticket-of-leave they were promised for volunteering, after a period of service. On the face of it, this was a good offer because ticket-of-leave holders had the right to work for themselves and had some freedom of movement. At Melville Island, this wasn't as gracious as it sounded because there wasn't anywhere else to go. However, if they held a ticket-of-leave, it meant they were paid for their work at the fort and they could then purchase more from the commissariat or visiting ships, which made life more comfortable.

When Campbell was in charge, he introduced a complicated tiered work system. Ticket-of-leave holders were paid money for working on government projects and were allowed to 'employ' ordinary convicts, depending on the amount of work they needed to do [60]. Campbell set work targets for the convicts—for example a sawyer needed to produce 200-250 feet of wood per week, slab splitters needed to make sixty slabs a day, and dirt carriers had to fill and empty their handcarts every thirty minutes over a quarter of a mile, with an additional ten minutes for each quarter mile. How he managed to supervise and evaluate such precise measurements is unknown. Convicts had to work from sunrise till sunset, except for a four-hour break in the middle of the day. Also, Captain Barlow had only expected the convicts to work in dry weather, not in the rain, and Campbell carried this tradition on.

Convicts were paid for their labour in both cash and commodities from the commissariat store. Barlow dispensed payment four times a year, paying six months' worth of commodities in the first and third quarters and cash in the other two. Convicts could receive two shillings a day and use it to purchase food and other items, or one shilling per day plus rations. Campbell's system was to pay ticket-of-leave holders a shilling a day, when they worked on government projects, and full rations on every day of the year. Ordinary convicts were paid less. There was almost no other way of earning money, like in larger settlements, because there was no other industry or commerce available on the island. The exception to this, of course, was the smuggling and reselling of alcohol bought from visiting ships, and a few individuals probably profited from this, but others were caught and lost privileges as a result.

Some prisoners were near the end of their sentences and were fortunate to be given a passage back to Sydney before their time expired. John Parry was one who returned to Sydney in August 1828, because his sentence expired on 22 October, and he was then a free man.

58

Record keeping by the court system was much better than that of the military so there are biographies of nearly all the convicts who worked at the remote settlements, including their crimes, court statements, and sentences (see Appendix 4). Unfortunately, little information exists about the soldiers, sailors, or marines, some of whom travelled with their wives and children.

Some people arrived, fell sick, and died. Fourteen prisoners died from scurvy, or other diseases, and attacks from the Tiwi. The first to die was Joseph Lorien, just days after the British arrived, when he was poisoned by fruit he ate in the bush. Others survived but were invalided out. Some worked at the fort for the entire time it existed, and two even returned there to work as free men. A few were transferred to Fort Wellington after Fort Dundas closed and had to endure another six months until they were returned to Sydney (see Appendix 6).

The commandants naturally mentioned many convicts in their reports and diaries, and diligent historians have been able to trace the lives of many that survived after they had returned to Sydney from Melville Island. Street for example, gathered data from the court records like this:

"William Roberts: age 17 years; native place, Liverpool; trade, turner apprentice 3 years; height 5 ft 2 ½ ins; year born, 1802; race, Mulatto; complexion, black; eyes, black; hair, black; marks, pock marked. Man and Anchor, WR, heart and wreath on lower left arm. Scars on right cheek bone."[132]

Roberts had stolen a watch from a 'boot closer' named Edward Nelson on Drury Lane and was sent to the penal colonies for fourteen years, which included several years on Melville Island. He earned his freedom in 1834 in Sydney and married Hannah Sullivan at St Andrews Church in 1840, when he was thirty-eight years old and she was twenty. Despite her youth, poor Hannah had already lost her front teeth, had a diagonal scar across her nose, and the nail on the third finger of her right hand was split.

William was little more than a child. Short, brown-skinned, and already a third year apprentice, he had survived small pox and, judging by the wreath tattooed on his arm, had already seen his share of tragedy.

Many of the descriptions of convicts contain a lot of detail, and they give life to long forgotten names. They stand in contrast to the paucity of information about other men, women, and children who called Fort Dundas home. It is the stories about those individuals who made a large contribution or had a significant influence on the Fort, those who did interesting things, and of course, those individuals who got into trouble, which helps us flesh out the participants and understand a little of the society of the settlement.

The current community of Pirlangimpi stands on the land cleared by settlers for use as a garden. It was called, simply enough, *Garden Point*, a name the Catholic Church retained when it started a mission there in 1941.

The convicts had begun clearing for agriculture as soon as possible after their arrival, near a small stream known as Johns River, after Captain Johns of the *Lady Nelson*, and a billabong that provided the gardens with water. However, the convicts lacked knowledge of the local soils, plants, and how best to grow them so their success was minimal. When the health of the soldiers and convicts began to deteriorate, Captain Barlow was concerned. When scurvy appeared among some of the men, something clearly had to be done. Barlow sent to Sydney for a professional gardener.

The man they found was a convict named John Matthew Richardson His record describes him as five-feet-six inches tall with hazel grey eyes, light brown hair, and a sallow complexion. He sported a number of tattoos on his arms.

Richardson was a second time convict—he had already spent four years in Sydney, from 1817, for stealing three gallons of gin, but had returned to England with a full pardon, earned by his participation in an expedition with John Oxley. He had been in charge of the collection of seeds and plants.

Back in England in 1822, he was again arrested after being caught house breaking. He was then twenty-seven-years-old and sentenced to death, but instead was once again transported, this time for the term of his natural life. A trained gardener was much needed in the colonies, and when he arrived in Hobart in 1822 with 153 other prisoners, his skill was immediately called upon. He was assigned to a Mr Gerriott as a gardener in Hobart, but this wasn't to last. Despite Gerriott trying to keep him, he was shipped to Sydney and appointed overseer of the Government Gardens there.

Richardson seems to have been well respected, because he accompanied John Oxley on another expedition in 1823 and perhaps again in 1824 to Moreton Bay as a plant collector and assistant to the botanist Alan Cunningham. Life was good for a while, though still a convict, he married a free-woman named June Nelson in July 1824, and they soon had their first child.

Barlow needed a gardener on Melville Island and the Government was offering tickets of leave for convicts who would volunteer for the role. Richardson was encouraged to apply and was quickly accepted. In November, 1825, a letter from the Engineer's Office in Sydney tells us:

"Richardson, the prisoner, who proceeds in charge of the plants and seeds from the Botanical Gardens is to receive a salary of £25* per annum from the 16th inst. And £10 have been paid him in advance to enable him to procure the necessary comforts for himself and family during the voyage."

*   £25 in 1824 is equivalent to about $1250 nowadays.

John, June, and their small child were then shipped to Melville Island on the *Sir Phillip Dundas*, arriving there in February 1826. By March, he complained that he had not been given rations for his wife and child, nor was he allocated a dwelling as promised. As they had arrived at the height of the wet season and were raising a small child with insufficient food and only a canvas tent to call home, there must have been good grounds for his complaints, but it remained this way for more than a year. During that year the workload was punishing, and at one point Richardson was sent to Timor in the cutter *Mermaid* to collect plants and seeds from the Dutch Resident.

Richardson earned his £25: growing enough vegetables for over a hundred settlers in poor soils and in a climate, which was hot and very dry, unless it was hot and very wet, was a major challenge. However, he was reasonably successful, as the scourge of scurvy at the fort lessened.

In March 1827, June gave birth to her second child, Elizabeth Melville Richardson. Elizabeth was the first Caucasian child born in North Australia.

Then, by May 1827, June's health began to deteriorate and it was arranged for her and the children to be shipped back to Sydney on the *Amity*. Unfortunately, Richardson spoiled this by getting into trouble for buying $150 of spirits from the sailors of a visiting ship and then selling it on to soldiers and convicts for $300. This so annoyed Major Campbell that he cancelled June's passage to Sydney as a punishment, even though June was a free woman. They had to wait more than eighteen months after that for the fort to be closed down to return to Sydney in the *HMS Lucy Ann* with the troops and other convicts that weren't transferred to Fort Wellington. June's health never improved and she died on 31 July 1830, aged forty-three years. A note was attached to her death certificate: 'she had been sick at Melville Island but refused passage to Sydney.'[132]

John was given a ticket-of-leave on 21 September 1829, and when June died, he was left to raise the children. In February

1831, his ticket was cancelled for poor behaviour: he fell repeatedly into trouble for drunkenness, and he was punished by short periods in the cells. As well, he was given twenty-five lashes in 1832, and twenty-five and fifty lashes on separate occasions in 1834, for absconding.

It was not until 1837 that John finally got his life together and he earned a conditional pardon from Governor Sir Richard Bourke. Richardson attended Sir Thomas Mitchell's expedition in 1836, as botanical collector and discovered sixty-eight new species. Mitchell praised his 'indefatigable industry on this expedition, although an old man' (he was thirty-nine) and made representations on his behalf. After fifteen years as a convict, Richardson was finally a free man. He worked with plants for the remainder of his life—a few like *Hibiscus richardsonii* and *Alyxia richardsonii* are named after him. He died in 1882 at the age of eighty-five, sufficiently respected enough to earn a place in the *Australian Dictionary of Biography* [8].

Richardson had a protégé in the gardens—an assistant called William (aka Michael) McCarthy. McCarthy was fourteen years old when he was tried and found guilty of the crime of stealing a handkerchief valued at five shillings. His defence was 'I found it!' but he and a mate were sentenced to be transported 'beyond the seas' for life. He was a plasterer's boy and gardener. Grey eyed, with a ruddy, pockmarked face, and brown hair, he came from London and landed in Sydney in May 1821. He volunteered for Fort Dundas in November 1825 and arrived on the *Sir Phillip Dundas*. He appears briefly in the hospital records a couple of times—once for colic and once for scurvy. For two years, he kept out of trouble and was a good worker in the gardens. Major Campbell thought highly of him. He was therefore recommended to be the gardener at the new Raffles Bay settlement of Fort Wellington. Campbell told Captain Smythe that McCarthy would be the 'proper person to send down' and was the only man who could tend a garden, besides Richardson. In convict terms, this must have seemed like a promotion.

McCarthy prospered and earned his ticket-of-leave in 1830. After his return to Sydney, he lived in Liverpool and died there in 1865, aged fifty-nine years.

Two female convicts were sent to Fort Dundas during its existence. Jane Baker, aged thirty-three years, was serving fourteen years for larceny and was assigned as a servant to Mr Walker, caring for Mrs Walker and their small child. Walker was the master of the *Amity*.

Jane arrived late in the life of the settlement, in 1828, when the *Amity* was stationed at Fort Dundas. Unfortunately, she became embroiled in a conflict that arose between Mrs Walker and the Commandant, when the officers of the ship were drawn into violent quarrels with the men. History doesn't record what the quarrels were about, but Mrs Walker was blamed and she was ordered ashore with her children and Jane, because their presence aboard was 'to the detriment of the Public Service.'[107]

Jane's was a hard life. After her time at Melville Island, she was transferred to the Female Factory at Parramatta and she died there soon after, aged thirty-six years. Her worldly goods (two gowns, two petticoats, two shifts, three caps, three handkerchiefs, one pair of stays, and one silk bonnet) were auctioned there in March of 1831, raising a total of six shillings and five pence.

Mary Ann Rycroft, also known as Diane Hughes, arrived in Sydney in 1825, aged thirty-eight years, on a life sentence for stealing about six pounds worth of clothing. She was a London dressmaker and servant who was five-feet-two and a quarter inches tall, with hazel eyes and a sallow complexion. Mary Ann was initially sentenced to be hanged in Newgate Prison, but instead, she was shipped out for life 'beyond the seas' to the colony on the transport ship *Midas*, with 109 other women.

The arrival of a ship full of women always caused excitement among the lonely men of Sydney, and Mary Ann was quickly courted and won by William Moxham, a blacksmith. Together they took up an offer of work in the new settlement and arrived in Fort Dundas in September 1828 for the last few months of its existence. They helped pack it up and were shipped on the *Amity* to Fort Wellington. Captain Hartley was on the same ship—the very last transport off the island on 14 February 1829. The Moxhams and eleven other prisoners stayed at Fort Wellington where Mary Ann fell into a nursing role of the sick and dying. She also had to wash and lay out the dead for burial.

Mary Ann had earned her ticket-of-leave when she returned to Sydney, but lost it when she was convicted of drunkenness and disorderly conduct and spent two months in the Female Factory at Parramatta in 1837. She finally won it back and was allowed to live and work in Sydney where she died, in 1857, aged sixty-nine years.

October is a hot month in the tropical north. The humidity is continuously high, but it rains only occasionally, as the wet season, still weeks away, teases and flirts with the thirsty bush. A cloud formation, known nowadays as 'Hector,' builds up every day above the centre of Melville Island, promising rain. It is such a reliable weather phenomenon that lightning scientists come from across the world to study it. But Hector is often full of empty promises, for only when the monsoon actually arrives do the clouds release their bounty to fill the creeks and rejuvenate the forests.

Living at Fort Dundas, the settlers suffered in the oppressive heat and humidity, watching Hector form and blow away every afternoon, hoping that rain would come to break the 'build-up.' But rain or no rain, the struggle for survival meant that there was always work to do.

One morning near the end of October 1826, two convicts, Julius Campbell and Edward Lowther, were sent out towards the gardens to cut grass fodder for the penned animals near the fort. Campbell was an old hand, having served at Fort Dundas since its beginning. He had generally been a good worker and was trusted enough to be carrying a musket for protection, if needed. A Jamaican ship's steward, he was transported for seven years for stealing clothing in Liverpool during 1822. As a skilled black man, he was a favoured volunteer for Fort Dundas because the Government believed that Africans would do better work and survive the rigours of the climate better than other races. In fact, most Europeans of the time thought that Africans were more suited to a tropical climate than other races, and thirteen of the convicts that served at the fort over the years were of African descent [60]. Campbell had stayed only about a month in Sydney, as he was quickly recruited and sent on the *Countess of Harcourt*.

Edward Lowther, at twenty-four, was ten years younger than Campbell but had already served more than a year at the settlement. He had been convicted of highway robbery, after robbing a man in Lancashire, and had earned himself transportation for fourteen years in 1824. He was a sawyer and a 'wet cooper,' a trade that was very useful to the new settlement, so he, like Campbell, was accepted quickly and thus spent very little time in Sydney. The Commandant recorded what happened one morning about two years after the fort area was settled:

"At 9am on Thurs 26/10/1826 Campbell and Lowther left Fort Dundas to cut grass. They were attacked by the Tiwi. Campbell carried a musket. Lowther hooks for cutting grass. Campbell died with three spears sticking in him. Lowther was grazed."[33]

Major Campbell's uncharacteristically short report was fleshed out

66

during an enquiry he held later that day with the help of Assistant Surgeon Gold. Their minutes survive in the State Records of New South Wales*. Edward Lowther was interviewed first:

"We had not gone far distant... when we saw a number (I suppose 20) of natives painted in various parts of their bodies and armed with waddies. I asked Campbell if we should go back again? He answered 'No, they may go away'. We went on, losing sight of the natives until we came to a bridge which leads to a swamp about half a mile from the settlement. We passed over it, and had proceeded some paces when we again saw the natives. Campbell and myself instantly stopped, beckoning, and making other signs, which we usually made when we wished them to go away. They did not however take any notice of them but approached us shaking their waddies and spears, and hallooing and jumping about in a threatening manner. As they came near, Campbell presented his musket at them and snapped twice, but the musket would not go off. We then ran away as fast as we could towards the bridge which we recrossed closely pursued by the natives. I ran faster than Campbell. Several waddies fell near me, and one spear struck me on the thigh, but it did not hurt me. When some distance from the bridge, I suppose about three hundred yards, I looked behind me and I saw the natives so close to Campbell that they could strike him with a spear without letting go out of their hands. On looking forward I saw John Westwood coming quickly towards me from the direction of the settlement armed with a musket. I then stood still and looking round saw the natives run away and Campbell fall."

Lowther then hurried to get Assistant Surgeon Gold whilst John Westwood went to Campbell's aid. Westwood was quick and well-armed, and the Tiwi did not wait to reckon with him, but

---

* *Attack by Aborigines*, State Record of New South Wales: Copy of Document 245, 1825

he could do nothing:

> *"I ran to Campbell, who was then standing; his head was leaning towards one side and as I looked at him he fell but never spoke. I passed Campbell a few paces after the natives who were running away, but thinking it imprudent to follow them I went back to him and found him dead. He had three spears sticking in his body."*

Lowther was no doubt shaken by his ordeal, but he survived his time at Fort Dundas and was finally freed in Sydney at the end of his sentence in 1839. John Westwood, a sugar and cheese thief from Scotland, also survived and was one of those invalided back to Sydney by Captain Hartley and Assistant Surgeon Sherwin in September 1828. He had earned his ticket-of-leave on Melville Island, and a few years later, in 1835, was granted a conditional pardon, having served sixteen years of his life sentence.

Living in the Fort cannot have been easy on the nerves. Much land had been cleared, but the huts and the hospital were still too close to the trees. The forest was thick in parts, and it provided good cover for clever Tiwi men. They had honed their hunting skills since childhood to remain unseen by magpie geese and wallabies, so stalking the Englishmen was no doubt less of a challenge. The Tiwi could watch the settlement quietly, get within a spear throw of the huts, and wait for their chance to send one flying. Sometimes a spear would fly straight through open windows or doorways. Many caused no damage, but a few of the settlers were hit and wounded.

Forty-year-old Henry Taylor was one man who was hit by a spear. Convicted of larceny in 1808 and sentenced to death, his sentence was later changed to transportation for life. Taylor had arrived in Sydney in 1810, and had been awarded and then lost several tickets-of-leave. The opportunity to serve in Fort Dundas, earn, and perhaps keep, for once, another ticket-of-leave was very attractive, so he volunteered for Melville Island and sailed there in May 1826 in the *Mermaid*. Taylor was a man who seems to have been in and out of trouble his whole life, but he clearly behaved himself at Fort Dundas and is hardly mentioned in reports. But, on 18 July 1827, he was inside the settlement and, without warning, was hit by a carefully aimed Tiwi spear. Wounded in the leg, he had several weeks' recuperation in the settlement hospital, before returning to work, no doubt nervously looking over his shoulder more often than before.

Unfortunately for him, and perhaps characteristically, when he returned to Sydney, Taylor started once again to get into trouble. He was convicted of larceny in Parramatta in 1836 and sentenced to a year in irons. In 1843, he was granted his freedom, but four years later he was declared insane and was sent to the Convict Lunatic Asylum in Parramatta for two years. He was discharged in 1849 and died a few months later.

Joseph Lorien stole an axe and other woodworking tools from a wheelwright and was sentenced to seven years transportation in 1822. Lorien was a labourer of African descent and was one of the thirteen black convict volunteers chosen to be sent to the northern settlement. Unfortunately, his life there was cut short soon after the *Countess of Harcourt* landed him.

The anonymous officer who provided his journal to *The Australian* wrote on 1 October 1824*:

> *"Labour of clearing resumed. Some hands procuring water. Serjeant (sic) Stewart and Joseph Loraine, missing; the latter a man of colour,*

---

* Note: Street[132] incorrectly lists him as lost on 10 March 1827.

and a prisoner. A corporal and two men went in search of the lost, but were unsuccessful.

> *Oct. 2.—This morning Serjeant Stewart returned alone; the unfortunate black by eating some of the berries which grow on the sago tree*, having become so dreadfully afflicted with a retching pain, as to be unable to proceed any farther on his way back. The serjeant after travelling all night returned without him, having left him a large kangaroo dog, two pheasants, and a hatchet. The luckless negro is never more heard of."*

Lorien was lost in the bush, poisoned, but his body was never found. Sergeant Henry Stewart estimated that he'd left him asleep or unconscious fifteen miles from camp, but the search parties that were sent out to find him failed. There are no 'sago' palms on Melville Island so it is likely he actually ate the poisonous fruit of the local cycad. The dog was never found either, but as Campbell put it: 'the saurian order are also very numerous.' Roe also reported the death, the fifth since they had left Sydney (after the four who drowned at Port Essington):

> *"...poor Lorraine (sic) and the dog never made their appearance, and various, of course, are the conjectures as to what may have been their ultimate fate."* [114]

Escape from Melville Island was a daunting proposition. The convicts

---

* The cycad, which is toxic, is common on Melville Island. Roe called it *Cycas circinalis,* but these days it is known as *Cycas armstrongii,* named after John Armstrong, who was a collector and gardener at Victoria Settlement. Armstrong collected more than a 1,000 specimens in the Cobourg area. *Cycas armstrongii* is one of about seven species that were named after him. As a food, it needs to be prepared carefully and this includes leaching in water over several days. It was also used as a bush medicine when mixed with urine as an antiseptic for spear wounds[28].

would have had little idea where in the world they actually were and in which direction possible freedom lay. However, there were those who were not deterred by the prospect of being lost at sea, and plans were made, which included the secret construction of a boat, until, on 26 April 1828, two men risked their health and safety by becoming snitches. The first was John Daniel Jones Probyn, a break-and-enter burglar who had stolen enough clothing to earn himself a fourteen-year sentence of transportation beyond the seas. He was a twenty-year-old carpenter from Bristol with pale skin, brown eyes, a large nose, and a scar on his forehead. He arrived in Sydney in March 1824 and was one of the first prisoners to volunteer for duty at Fort Dundas. He was shipped in the *Countess of Harcourt* and had survived the occasional bout of scurvy, and once he was hospitalised after 'punishment,' but generally he kept himself quite healthy.

The other was John Francis who was on a life sentence for 'larceny in a dwelling.' He was a twenty-four-year-old black labourer from St Vincent in the West Indies who had been granted a ticket-of-leave by Captain Barlow in 1825. Campbell described him as a 'very industrious man' who had 'generally conducted himself well during the time he has been on Melville Island.'

In an interview with Major Campbell, Probyn and Francis formally dobbed in some fellow convicts who were planning an escape:

> *"I, John Probyn, do make oath that I saw John Westward[†],… talking to Sowerby and Oakley[‡], two prisoners of the Crown… the day on which the boat, that was built by some prisoners clandestinely in the bush, was launched and in which they*

[†] John Westward was one of the prisoners invalided back to Sydney due to ill health by **Assistant Surgeon** Sherwin in August 1828.

[‡] Henry Oakley was named by the magistrates as among those who intended to escape, but no punishment is recorded. Assistant Surgeon Sherwin invalided him back to Sydney due to ill health in August 1828.

71

intended attempting to escape. Charles Wilson*, a prisoner of the crown, told me on Monday morning, the 14th April, in the presence of John Parry†, that the boat was 21 feet long, that he had run great risks several nights in working at her, that it would be great murder for it to be found out, that he would not give a halfpenny or that anyone's life, who informed about it, would not be worth a halfpenny. Charles Holt, a prisoner of the Crown, had come to eat his victuals at the same hut or house with Parry and myself, about a week previous to the Amity's arrival on the 8th of April. In conversing about us being relieved from Sydney, Parry observed that it would not be long before 5 or 6 men would be off from this place on the boat they were building, and observed that a noise, which had been heard amongst the mangroves some time previous by some bark strippers (among which I was) and which noise was took for the Natives, was made by Charles Wilson and the Stock keepers in building a boat. Parry also said that he understood that a handsaw, which he had lost, was out at the place where the boat was building. I told Parry that I knew where the noise was made and could find the place. Consequently Parry and myself went out on Monday morning, the 14th April, and found the boat and several tools, and amongst them the handsaw which Parry had lost. On the same day when we returned home, Holt seeing the saw, told me that Wilson had frequently asked him to join in building the boat. Holt said that Wilson would frequently go out of a moonlight night with a pistol and alone for the purpose of building the boat. Sowerby was out one day at the boat and I saw him late in the afternoon with his trousers covered in swamp dirt.... Parry who was in possession of the particulars of the intended escape of the prisoners before

---

*   Charles Wilson: This is the only reference to a convict named Charles Wilson at Fort Dundas. There is no further information about him, except that he may have been the 'ship's carpenter' mentioned by Campbell elsewhere.

†   Soon after this, John Parry's sentence expired and he was returned to Sydney in September 1828.

*I was, told me that the prisoners were Martin the Blacksmith, who had made the ironwork for the boat, Sellers‡, and Phillips§, Sowerby¶, Chas. Wilson and Evans.***"* [132]

Campbell immediately held an investigation and brought together a Bench of Magistrates to examine the evidence and interview all involved. The boat builders must have hidden or destroyed the boat, because the magistrates found that they had to acquit Charles Wilson and the others for lack of evidence with no punishment. This seems an extraordinary outcome, but Campbell may have been tired, or his mind may have been on other things as, in the same week, Hartley had arrived to relieve him. Wilson and the others may have been lucky.

Probyn, however, was scared for his life. Campbell wrote in his dispatch to Colonial Secretary McLeay that Probyn was:

"…so much in dread of suffering some serious bodily injury, that I was obliged to allow him to live in the Military Barracks. In consideration of the information which Probyn had given, probably at the hazard of his life, I conceived he had a claim for protection and indulgence, and have therefore ordered him a passage on board the Governor Phillip to Sydney…" [33]

The *Governor Phillip* took Francis to Sydney as well, as he had been also 'marked down as an object of revenge when opportunity offers' [37]. Both Francis and Probyn lived a few more years in New South

---

‡   Matthew Sellers, a seaman, was later transferred to Raffles Bay, and was found to be preparing another escape in August 1829 and was placed under guard by Commandant Barker.

§   William Phillips later served in Raffles Bay and had his escape attempt also foiled by Commandant Barker–he and others were planning to steal a schooner or whaleboat.

¶   John Sowerby returned to Sydney in the *Isabella* on 28 January 1828. If this is true, he could not have been building a boat in April 1828 on Melville Island.

**   No convict named Evans is listed in the records for Fort Dundas.

Wales. Francis died in Goulburn in 1840, aged forty-eight years. Probyn* was listed in the NSW Government Gazette on 5 July 1837 among those granted their Certificates of Freedom and from there disappears from the record.

Drunkenness and the thirst for beer, rum and gin, are a common theme between both the military and the convicts at Fort Dundas. Reading the biographies of convicts, the tickets-of-leave they earned were often disqualified through drunken behaviour.

John Simpson was a convict with a seven-year sentence who signed up at the first opportunity for the new settlement, and travelled with the founders on the *Countess of Harcourt* in 1824. He seems to have kept out of trouble for more than three years and had been granted his ticket-of-leave by Captain Barlow in 1825. Then, in December 1827, he was caught stealing a pint of spirits from the commissariat.

It seems that Simpson was able to draw off a pint of liquor (worth 7 ½ pence) whilst William Ladbrook, the Stores Issuer, was in the loft locking the two double windows. Simpson was spotted by Private William Dyer of the 57th Regiment with something under his jacket, and Dyer informed his superior, Corporal Thomas Allen. Simpson at first denied hiding anything, then offered to give the bottle to the soldiers because he didn't have any money. Campbell, in his role as Justice of the Peace, deliberated and gave his judgement:

> *"I am of the opinion that the said John Simpson abstracted spirits from his Majesty's Magazines in a fraudulent and clandestine manner on the afternoon of the 13th instant… In consequence of this finding I do hereby deprive John Simpson of his Ticket-of-leave until such*

---

* Probyn lost his ticket-of-leave for drunkenness in 1830 (*The Sydney Monitor* 21 July 1830).

time as the pleasure of his Excellency the Governor of New South Wales and its dependencies is made known."[132]

Simpson returned to Sydney and had his ticket-of-leave renewed in August 1828 and his sentence expired soon after. As a free man, he married in Bathurst in 1831.

Life at Fort Dundas was clearly difficult. Monotonous work, poor diet and living conditions, and the stress of being at war with the Tiwi must have been a trial. Despite this, two men, William Spowage and Thomas Cox, elected to stay and work as free men at Fort Dundas after their sentences expired, earning salaries.

Thomas Cox landed in Sydney for a seven-year sentence in June 1822, working as a blacksmith there for several years. He was married in June 1823, but when he volunteered to go to Melville Island on the *Sir Phillip Dundas* in November 1825, his wife was not mentioned.

Cox was a metalworker, and his skills were much in demand at the Fort when he gained his freedom in April 1827. So, instead of jumping on the first transport out, he stayed on Melville Island as a paid worker. Later, when he could afford to pay his way, he travelled to Timor looking for work, but when he couldn't find any, he returned to Fort Dundas and worked there for a while longer before getting transport to Sydney in June 1827, working his passage as a sailor on the *Isabella*.

William Spowage also had a seven-year sentence (for stealing a handkerchief), and he arrived in 1821 at the age of sixteen years. He was a boat builder, and he signed for Melville Island at the same time as Thomas Cox and travelled with him on the *Sir Phillip Dundas* in November 1825. Spowage was recorded as returning to Sydney on the *Mermaid* on 22 May 1826, but he was back in

Fort Dundas before November 1828 as a free man, employed as a respected tradesman.

Walter Wilson was a twenty-seven-year old Coldstream Guard court-marshalled for setting fire to a room in Cambrai, France, where he had been as a part of the post-war occupation force. He was found guilty and sentenced to fourteen years transportation. In Sydney, he volunteered his services with the first group to go to Melville Island and worked his way to becoming a convict overseer by 1827. He had problems, however, as Campbell wrote in his sixth dispatch to Colonial Secretary McLeay:

> *"I am much in want of a proper person to assist, or fill the situation of Overseer. The present one (Wilson) is a very hardworking attentive man, but much addicted to liquor, which notwithstanding my utmost endeavours is sometimes introduced from on board vessels. He has frequently expressed a desire to give it up; but I am obliged to retain him as there is not a single person here I could trust. His duties are very severe and it requires an active able man to perform them. I therefore solicit that someone capable of succeeding him be sent down, and whom I can appoint should it be necessary."* [37]

Wilson did not succeed in giving up liquor. One day, the *Amity* was moored off the jetty with the crew unloading stores. Wilson claimed that at some time during the day he organised a deal with the captain, Mr Owen, to purchase a bottle of rum and some sugar. Plagued by bad luck, Wilson was caught after dark by the sentries, Corporal Thomas Foley and Private George Rowe, trying to 'borrow' a small dinghy to row out to the *Amity* to pick up his purchase.

On 6 August 1828, Commandant Hartley and Lieutenant John Ovens, the Justices of the Peace in the settlement, conducted

76

a hearing. Wilson was found guilty as charged, and as punishment, he lost his status as overseer and had his ticket-of-leave suspended for six months. During that time, he had to 'work with the Crown Prisoners not holding tickets-of-leave.'[66]

Wilson returned to Sydney at the close of the settlement and was granted freedom at the end of his sentence in 1832. He settled in the lower Hawkesbury Valley and married Ann Rowland; although, sadly, she died only two years later.

The hospital records and the list of deaths in the settlement show that scurvy was a major problem, as already noted. Many convicts are recorded as having this illness at one time or other, though most of them recovered. Some were sent back to Sydney on the *Isabella* when it brought the relieving garrison in December 1826. Over the years, the death rate dropped, but this was not necessarily because the scourge of scurvy had been beaten. Rather, by 1828, many of those too sick to work were identified and invalided back to Sydney. Assistant Surgeon Sherwin wrote of them:

> *"I certify that the health of these men is so generally deranged as to render their removal from this settlement highly advisable. I do not however think that their remaining here during the dry season will, in any way, increase their present indisposition. But I am of the opinion that another wet season will, in all probability prove fatal to them."* [132]

It took a long time, as permission had to be gained from the Colonial Secretary, but finally, Captain Hartley was able to send the invalids away:

> *"...pursuant to your instructions... I shall forward to Headquarters per Governor Phillip the Crown Prisoners named in the margin. Their several cases being considered by Mr. Assistant Surgeon*

Sherwin of a nature to require their immediate removal from this unfriendly climate." [67]

These prisoners included Daniel Connor, Charlie Green, Jeremiah McCarthy, John Montgomery, William Lewis, James Tree, Henry Oakley, and John Westwood. Most were men who served their time quietly and were comparatively unremarkable. Some occasionally got into trouble for drunkenness or other crimes, but, thanks to Sherwin sending them back south, they survived their years on Melville Island and could continue healthier lives back in Sydney or Parramatta after their return.

As an example, Henry Oakley worked as a carpenter during most of the Fort's existence. He had made the mistake of stealing a fob-watch in London from a man who recognised him because he had known him for many years. For this, he was transported for the term of his natural life and he arrived in Sydney in October 1819, aged nineteen years. Five years later, with nothing to lose and a ticket-of-leave to gain, he volunteered for Melville Island as soon as it was advertised, knowing his skills in carpentry would be much in demand.

Oakley was named as one of those intending to attempt escape in April 1828, but he had often been sickly with 'contusions.' By June 1828, he was so ill that Assistant Surgeon Sherwin recommended his removal before he died. Captain Hartley agreed and Oakley was sent to Sydney with the others on the *Governor Phillip* in September 1828. His ticket of leave, granted for his services on Melville Island, was quickly cancelled and torn up for 'neglect of muster and absconding from the district" of Parramatta. He later spent twelve months in chains for stealing and wasn't freed until 1850. He died three years later in Bathurst, aged fifty-four years. If he had escaped in a homemade boat from Fort Dundas as he'd planned, he may have died in the attempt, so his illness and suffering in Fort Dundas could have actually saved his life.

8

THE TIWI

Figure 8 Tiwi people using stringybark shelters, photographed in 1914 by Alfred Searcy121

The Tiwi of Melville and Bathurst Islands are members of several groups spread across the islands. According to Hart and colleagues, the term 'Tiwi' means 'we, the only people,' which erroneously gives the impression that the Tiwi thought there was no one else. The islands are geographically isolated from, but within sight of, the mainland, across the Clarence Strait and the Vernon Islands. The Tiwi mostly remained separated from mainland Indigenous Australians, at least until around 1890, so their unique language and culture evolved in relative isolation.

To the Tiwi, new arrivals from faraway lands, with undreamt of technologies, strange foods, and alien culture must have seemed strange and threatening. But as we only have written records from the British and, earlier on, the Dutch, what the Tiwi actually thought is not recorded.

Early foreign visitors include Pieter Pieterszoon, commander of the ships *Cleen, Amsterdam,* and *Wesel,* who sailed the northwest coast of Melville Island in 1636. He knew there was land there because a fellow Dutchman had seen the islands in 1623, and Pieterszoon's three ships spent nine days exploring the northern coast. The crew saw campfires on the shore but did not meet any people.

A few years later, Abel Tasman visited the islands twice, in 1642 and 1644, unsuccessfully looking for new routes or new countries with which the Dutch could trade. The first recorded contact with the Tiwi, however, was made by another Dutchman, Maarten van Delft, in 1705. The three ships under van Delft's command, *de Vossenboch, Waaier,* and *Nova Hollandia* spent two weeks surveying the north coast of Melville Island, Apsley Strait, and most of Bathurst Island. In April 1705, they landed on Cape Van Diemen on Melville Island, now the site of the community of Milikapiti. At first, the Tiwi resisted the Dutch explorers, but relations improved to such an extent that the Dutch invited the Tiwi aboard their vessels [65] and they traded small items: the Tiwi offered fish and crabs while the Dutch provided clothing, ornaments, trade knives, and hatchets. The Tiwi also showed the Dutch a source of fresh water and allowed them to explore parts of the island. The two groups got on well until a conflict regarding articles of clothing split them up and the Dutch sailed away [57].

The Dutch weren't the only visitors: a few Macassan trepang fishermen, known to the British as "Malays," arrived and camped on parts of the north coast over a number of seasons. Several trepang cooking sites and *Tamarind* trees mark their old campsites, but mostly the Malays avoided Melville Island and generally fished along the coast of Arnhem Land. Searcy wrote in 1909 that the Malays had never managed to make friends on Melville like they had with tribes farther east.

In fact, by 1824, the Tiwi had a reputation as an unwelcoming and fearsome tribe who were willing to repel all visitors. Why this was the case is a mystery, because in 1705, despite the argument over clothing, the Tiwi had been friendly. What had changed for the Tiwi to become so unfriendly and distrustful? Some historians believe it was a result of decades of raids from the Portuguese for slaves during the 1700s [65, 107]. Commandant Campbell thought that the slavers were Malays, but, whoever they were, it appears that the raids finished around 1800. By then, though, the damage to international relationships had already been done.

Few other visitors came: Nicholas Baudin, a Frenchman, mapped the southwestern tip of Bathurst Island in 1802, but he never landed and avoided meeting any of the Tiwi at all. Then, in 1818, Phillip Parker King undertook a detailed survey of most of the two islands. He landed on Luxmore Head, accompanied by John Septimus Roe and the botanist Alan Cunningham, on 17 May. They were just starting some preliminary surveying when a small party of armed Tiwi surprised them. They made a hasty retreat to get back to their boat where there were some armed sailors, and in the rush, King left his theodolite tripod behind. Afterwards, he attempted to negotiate for the tripod's return in exchange for a few axes. He returned to the beach with several armed men and met a party of twenty-two Tiwi men and three women who had gathered on the shoreline. In a friendly gesture, an old man waded out to the boat and dropped a basket on the deck before hurrying back to the beach. It contained food and some water, and King threw him a hatchet in return. Then they were encouraged to bring their boat closer to the beach by a woman, but, as they approached, King saw a group of armed men hiding in the mangroves and a couple of canoes nearby, so he ordered the boat off shore again.

The Tiwi started to perform a dance in the shallows and continued it over and over again until King was 'thoroughly disgusted with them, and felt a degree of distrust that could not be conquered.' King realised that the Tiwi had spears aplenty hidden in the sand and floating on the water, whilst pretending to be unarmed. He therefore decided to withdraw, leave the theodolite tripod behind and forget his survey of Luxmore Head [30]. Interestingly the Tiwi had motioned chopping to King, suggesting that they would exchange hatchets for water, thus showing that they already had experience of, and valued, metal tools [121, 57].

Six years later, when Bremer and the Fort Dundas settlers arrived on Luxmore Head, they met no one. Within a few days, they had moved south to Point Barlow, near the only source of fresh water they could find, and started clearing the forest. The Tiwi must have known they were there, of course: the ships' mastheads were higher than the trees and the sounds of axes and cannons carry far across water. No doubt they quickly realised the newcomers were intending to stay. Bremer knew what had happened to King and had the experienced John Septimus Roe to advise him. He was ready to trust no one and clearly knew the reputation of both the islanders to the north and those of Melville Island:

> " ...considering the known treachery of the Malays, and the numbers in which they come on to the Coast, as well as the probable hostility of the Natives, I determined I should be as strong as I could when circumstances render it." [24]

However, the Tiwi initially elected to stay away from the British; although their campfires were clearly visible at night, several kilometres down the strait. First contact was made on 25 October when Bremer took a party across to Bathurst Island to hunt birds or other game. While hunting, they stumbled upon a recent funeral site marked with the extraordinary carved and painted *pukumani* poles that are central to Tiwi funerary customs.

82

Whilst JS Roe sketched the scene, Bremer wondered at their 'simplicity and order,' which 'would not have disgraced a People much further advanced in intellectual endowment.' Campbell also described what they found:

> *"It appears to be the custom of the natives to bury their dead in retired spots near their most frequent camping ground. The burial place is circular, probably ten to twelve feet in diameter. It is surrounded by upright poles, many of which are formed at top like lances or halberds fourteen or fifteen feet high, and between these the spears and waddies of the deceased are stuck upright in the ground."* [33]

Figure 9 JS Roe's 1824 sketch of the 'pukumani' poles erected during a funeral on Bathurst Island.

Bremer was impressed. He could empathise with such an acknowledgement of a 'Superior Power' and thought that clearly the Tiwi people were 'by no means so rude and barbarous as those we have been accustomed to find amongst the New Hollanders generally'[24].

But their trespass upon a recent pukumani ceremony site might have caused some consternation among the Tiwi. The land here belonged to the Manauila band, as it still does today, and their response was to meet with Bremer's party as they returned in their boat downstream to the mouth of the creek. Eight or ten armed-men waited for them on a sandbank, and they seemed determined to prevent their exit. But,

83

as the boat came closer, the Tiwi withdrew to the shoreline where they threw down their spears and commenced haranguing the Englishmen, 'with loud and incessant talking and vehement gestures.'

Figure 10 A Pukumani mortuary ceremony photographed in the 1950s (State Library of South Australia)

To Bremer, it was an obvious provocation, but he was anxious to make friendly contact. When they were close enough, he ordered an oar to be held out towards the Tiwi, upon which he placed handkerchiefs and other trifles, which the Tiwi took (and discarded within minutes). Bremer was happy with the encounter, feeling that he had made some progress towards friendship, and boasted of the exchange at dinner on board the Tamar that night. His optimism was premature, however, because:

> *"Just as we had finished, and before the cloth was removed, they hailed us from Settlement, to say that the natives had come down and attacked them. We immediately armed and went on shore, and were told they had retreated into the woods, but had carried with them one of the marines."* [133]

Luckily, the story of the abduction was an exaggeration, but it set the scene for one of the more hopeful meetings the invaders had with the local men:

> *"… about half-a-mile from the Settlement (we) saw some of them retreating and looking behind; they stopped after we had followed for a short time, and came towards us making signs for us to go back. Capt. Bunn went a little forward from our party, and one of the natives also came forward, and after a little time was followed by the others; and they allowed some of us also to go towards them, and were shortly quite familiar, walking with us hand in hand. They came with us toward the Settlement but would not enter it. We made them a present of some handkerchiefs** which they seemed to care little for, but two or three hatchets being-given to them they were highly prized. Bread was offered them which some of them took, but they would not eat in any quantity, though we shewed them the*

---

*   There is some irony in the use of handkerchiefs as gifts–a number of the convicts on the island were only there because they had been convicted of stealing them."

example, and a surly suspicious looking dog made signs to me that it was poison, and would make him large bellied.

Walking in the woods next morning, I found the bread they kept, laid by the side of a fallen tree. There were eight or ten of them, good looking men, and were in size somewhat taller than a middling sized European; they had bushy beards and a robust appearance; quite naked, mid tattooed very prettily down the back and belly, and armed with spears and waddies very similar to those used by the natives in New South Wales. They were much struck with our clothes, which I believe, at first, they thought were a portion of our bodies; one of the party took off his shoes, which they seemed astonished at, and two or three wished to take off my boots, but they could not do it. When we were near the Settlement, our men came out to see the natives; and some of the prisoners who were men of colour with them, and having only then left their work, they had only their trousers on; our new made acquaintances were struck at their appearance, and made signs to them to take off their clothes, which one of them did, they shouting and examining him on all sides, and very much gratified to see him so much like themselves; they were very pressing for more axes (which they called 'peerces'), and stole one or two.

They left us towards sunset, laying their hands over their ears, and placing that side of their head towards the ground, which we interpreted as a sign, they were going to sleep." [133]

A couple of days later, the same anonymous officer had another positive meeting with some Tiwi men, this time on Bathurst Island:

"On the 27th, a boat from the Tamar having gone to Bathurst Island to fish, was met by another party of the natives, and in the evening we set sail for the place, in hopes of meeting them, but had only left the ship for a short time, when we discovered a fire which they had lighted to guide us. We went on shore there, and being among the first who landed I was presented with a dead owl on the

point of a spear, which I received as a token of good friendship; there were about seventeen men, and one female with a child at a little distance standing by a tree; she was a short woman, and as they seemed anxious to screen her, we did not go towards her; she had a mat hanging down from her middle to her knees; there was also a native dog with them, quite-tame. After mutual presents, we receiving waddies in exchange for old caps, bonnets, and handkerchiefs; and after leaving, in imitation of them, crossed our arms upon our breasts, beat our sides, danced and jabbered, we returned to our boats, and endeavoured to persuade one of them to go with us, but this we could not do; they seemed anxious for us to go away.

It appeared to me they were scarcely such stout men as those we had met on the Settlement side, but this might be from the circumstance of their being a whole tribe, while the others were merely a picked portion of one; they were similarly tattooed as the others, and one of them painted yellow on one side, and powdered on the head and beard with the same colour. Being fond of ornament, he was anxious to obtain my Leghorn bonnet, and begged hard for it. Some of them had their hair tied up behind as ornamental. An old grey haired and bearded man was chief, and seemed a good natured fellow; he came down to the water edge with us, and saw us off."[133]

Lieutenant John Septimus Roe wrote long letters to his father in which he described his early encounters with the Tiwi in letters:

"It was a long time before the natives made their appearance, though very large fires were visible on both shores, a few miles from the coast, brightening up immediately after each other, as if it for signals: at length a large party of them came down to the shore on both sides of the fort on the same day, and we had friendly communication with them, making them presents of hatchets, knives, beads, looking glasses, handkerchiefs, bread & anything we thought may amuse them, but received nothing in return – in fact they had nothing to

give, being destitute of any articles they might have bartered except spears and fighting clubs." [114]

Roe also noted that they weren't the only foreign visitors living on Melville Island:

"On the second day of their visit I was greatly astonished to see amongst them a young man of about twenty years of age, not darker in colour than a Chinese but with perfect Malay features and like all the rest entirely naked: he had daubed himself all over with soot and grease, to appear like the others, but the difference was plainly perceptible. On perceiving that he was the object of our conversation, a certain archness and lively expression came over his countenance, which a native Australian would have strained his features in vain to have produced. The natives appeared to be very fond of him. It seems probable that he must have been kidnapped when very young, or found while astray in the woods." [114]

The settlers quickly learned that the Tiwi didn't want the beads and handkerchiefs, or the strange English food, but they were very eager to get hold of some hatchets.

"They show no desire whatever for strange ornaments or trinkets. They are polite enough to accept of them without any expression of astonishment, but very soon afterwards take an opportunity of slyly dropping them or throwing them away. The only articles they seemed to covet were hatchets and other cutting tools; but when they could steal they carried off everything they could lay hold of." [33]

Cameron [30] says that the confrontation that developed between the Tiwi and the British may have been over property rights as much as an attempt to repel an invasion: the British had axes, and the Tiwi wanted them. The Tiwi felt that the British had an obligation to share as interlopers, and if they would not give them up freely, it was within

88

the Tiwi's rights to take them by force. Whatever the salient flashpoints between the two groups were, there were no more friendly exchanges:

> "They were all exceedingly clamourous for hatchets, which they called paaco-paaco, but having stolen several from Sawyers & men that were falling timber, these articles were invariably refused them until the stolen property was returned. With this arrangement they did not think proper to comply, and after the lapse of a week began open depredations on every one they met, taking the axes & knives & sickles of those men who were in the wood preparing materials for building, and raising their spears on the least symptom of resistance: This course of things could not of course be tolerated, and as an early lesson of our superiority would in all probability save much bloodshed, a guard was sent with every party thus employed, and resisted their attempts to rob. This induced the natives to throw their spears, and a musket was fired over their heads, but finding they were not hurt, their courage returned and their attacks were repeated, which made it necessary to fire at them, and they disappeared into the woods: Hostile proceedings having thus been commenced, every man going outside the settlement was armed, not less than two went together, and a guard … for the protection of the convicts." [114]

It took a month before the Tiwi were organised enough to try to repel the invaders. About one hundred warriors gathered on 30 October, and they attacked in two groups:

> "… upwards of sixty savages attacked a party of five marines who were cutting rushes for thatching, and two spears penetrated a bundle of them which one of the marines was carrying on his back. Their extreme cunning and slyness had enabled them to steal thus unperceived upon the marines, but their salute was promptly returned, and they were put to flight: followed upwards of a mile by nearly every man and dog in the settlement.

A party of about forty paid a similar visit to our watering place and garden and, dividing themselves into two parties under guidance of an old chief, surrounded 4 of our people that were haymaking, and four others that were watering with some small casks, under the direction of one of our young gentlemen. They closed so fast upon both parties, in defiance of the signs they made to keep off, and every man of them being armed with two or three spears, our people were obliged to fire over their heads to enforce attention. Unfortunately this had no further effect than lessening their former dread of what they now perceived could do them no harm, and they boldly advanced with their spears showing with such deliberate aim that one of them was shot dead at less than twelve yards distance*, in the act of discharging his weapon at our corporal. This had the momentary effect of checking their progress and of admitting our two parties to unite, when having only four muskets among them, and one of them useless, it was deemed prudent to re-embark and proceed on board the ship for assistance: this was finally effected in the midst of a shower of spears from the mangroves that line the beach, where the assailants had concealed themselves & which fortunately prevented their spears being discharged with formidable precision.

On the boat arriving on board the Tamar, which was at anchor a full mile from the scene of this affray, I proceeded immediately with an additional boat and eight men, armed, to recover our small casks, which to the number of thirty-two were left at the watering place in possession of the savages, but I was too late to gather even one small sprig of laurel on this occasion, the coast being quite clear, and presenting no impediment to the free embarkation of our water casks. We nevertheless reaped a harvest of spears and clubs which these scoundrels had left behind in the hurry of their flight, one of which was armed with no less than sixteen barbs and had penetrated the ground about nine inches. In general the spears of these people are not barbed, but are eight to ten feet in length, very sharply pointed,

---

* The shooter was Corporal Gwillan of the Marines, who was speared to death on 11/6/1825.

*well made, and are thrown by hand without aid of any stick, but
their fears prevented proper aim being taken, and though several
struck our people and fell into the boat, not one took effect."* [114]

The Tiwi withdrew, and despite the soldiers scouring the forest for
several kilometres around, nobody was seen for the remaining time
Bremer and Roe were at the settlement, and when they left, Roe was
confident that they had adequately demonstrated their superiority
and there would be no more major difficulty:

> *"The colonists, (in number about 100, including officers, military,
> convicts and 4 women) will have nothing to apprehend from any
> attacks by these people, except upon stragling (sic) individuals, in
> which they are capable of affording considerable annoyance by
> rendering it necessary to send a guard with every man that wants
> to cut thatching or wattles for the erection of his hut."* [114]

Why did it take more than a month before the first serious altercation
between the invaders and the invaded? Several reasons appear to be
likely. At first, the Tiwi might have been in awe of the technology they
could observe and the firepower that was demonstrated. They might
have withdrawn to observe, as they probably had for other powerful
visiting groups, hoping the newcomers would pack up and leave. But
when they saw the fort, the wharf, and dozens of huts being built, it
became clear that the British were intending to stay. The local band,
the Munupula, who owned the land that included *Punata*, which
the British called Point Barlow, would not have been large, and the
hundred or more armed men who were involved in the attacks of 30
October, could not have come from their number alone. It is likely
they sent runners to other bands, the Manauila from across the strait,
and their neighbours, the Mingwila and Wilrangwila, and called for
help. This conclusion is supported by the fact that the settlers saw few
Tiwi women, and only ever saw the men when they were fully armed [30].

91

Over the next four years, the Tiwi never sought friendship with the British, and neither side had any members who tried to learn the other's language. The Tiwi's coveted some of the invaders' belongings, but they weren't about to make any concessions to get them. And the changes to their lives brought by hatchets, buffalos, and pigs, took longer than the settlement existed – for example metal tools eventually allowed the Tiwi to copy Malay construction methods to make hollow log canoes [110].

In 1827, Commandant Campbell tried to break down the barriers a little by forcing one of the Tiwi to learn to speak English. The soldiers captured a man named Tambu Tipungwuti. It was thought that, if he could learn to speak English, he could order his people to stop stealing from the British, stop throwing spears at them, and to not kill their buffalo, or else the British would have to shoot them. Tambu was apparently chained and held captive in a hole in the ground, but the message was lost when he escaped after two weeks without learning to speak the foreigners' language. Not long afterwards, Assistant Surgeon Gold and Mr Green were speared to death, perhaps in revenge (see Chapter 5).

Grassby [64] concluded that, by 1827, the Tiwi had forced the garrison to stay within the fort and only leave it if they were ready for battle. He said the Tiwi's military tactics were 'sophisticated, effectively putting the fort under siege.' Thus, the garrison, a part of the most modern, effective and widespread empire the world had ever seen, was stymied. The Tiwi turned out to be excellent soldiers in the art of guerrilla warfare: Campbell called them 'revengeful, prone to stealing and in their attempts to commit depredations show excessive cunning, dexterity, arrangement, enterprise and courage.' [33].

Tiwi warriors could return to the fort and resume hostilities when other obligations were fulfilled or at their leisure. The British would spend weeks or months wondering when they would return, so to them it seemed a very piecemeal way of running a campaign. When they were in the area, the Tiwi would throw spears into the

92

buildings or the sawpits, steal axes and clothing, spear pigs, set fire to haystacks, break fences, and generally cause a pall of fear to descend across the settlers. Throwing their spears into the buildings was an 'expensive' exercise—spears and fighting sticks took time to make, and they could be lost after a single throw with no benefit, so clearly the resistance by the Tiwi was seen by them as a worthwhile investment to make against the invaders.

The most comprehensive, early description of the Tiwi comes from Major Campbell's 1834 presentation to the Royal Geographical Society in London. Written a number of years after his time at Fort Dundas, Campbell drew on his diaries and his memory and wrote several thousand words on all manner of aspects of the settlement. He was a career soldier but his anthropological interests were certainly admirable in his role of commandant. His description is a soldier's description, full of generalisations, but he does, nonetheless, present a broader understanding of the Tiwi than one might expect from an observer who, in reality, had very little contact with them:

> *"In personal appearance the natives of Melville Island resemble those of New Holland, and are evidently of the same stock; but they are more athletic, active and enterprising than those I saw on the south coast of Australia at Port Jackson, Newcastle, or Hunter River.*
>
> *They are not generally tall in stature, nor are they remarkable for small men. In groups of thirty I have seen five or six strong powerful men of six feet high, and some as short as five feet four or five inches. They are well formed about the body and thighs, but their legs are small in proportion, and their feet very large; their heads are flat and broad, with low foreheads, and the back of the head projects very much. Their hair is strong, like horse-hair, thick, curly or frizzled, and jet black. Their eye-brows and cheek-bones are extremely prominent; eyes small, sunk, and very bright and keen; nose flat and short; the upper lip thick and projecting; mouth remarkably large, with regular, fine white teeth; chin small, and face much contracted at bottom.*

93

They have the septum of the nose perforated, wear long, bushy beards, and have their shoulders and breasts scarified and raised in a very tasteful manner, and their countenance expresses good humour and cunning. All those who have reached the age of puberty are deficient in an upper front tooth, a custom common in New Holland.

The colour of their skin is a rusty black, and they go about perfectly naked. Their hair is sometimes tied in a knot, with a feather fixed in it, and they frequently daub it with a yellow earth. On particular occasions, when in grief, or intending mischief, or open hostilities, they paint their bodies, faces, and limbs with white or red pigments, so as to give themselves a most fantastic and even hideous appearance. In disposition they are revengeful, prone to stealing, and in their attempts to commit depredations show excessive cunning, dexterity, arrangement, enterprise, and courage. They are affectionate towards their children, and display strong feelings of tenderness when separated from their families. They are also very sensitive to anything like ridicule. They are good mimics, have a facility for catching up words, and are gifted with considerable observation. When they express joy they jump about, and clap their hands violently on their posteriors; and, in showing contempt, they turn their back, look over their shoulder, and give a smack upon the same part with their hand. In the construction of their canoes, spears, and waddies, they evince much ingenuity, although the workmanship is rough from the want of tools. They are expert swimmers and dive like ducks."

Campbell was, in the beginning, keen to be on good terms with the Tiwi, but he never managed to make much headway:

"When I assumed the command of the Island I was extremely anxious to court their friendship, as without it, with our limited means, we could never become acquainted with all the resources of the Island; but, notwithstanding, they continued until the last day distrustful, if not determinedly hostile. They put two gentlemen of

the settlement, one soldier, and one prisoner, to death, and wantonly wounded several others. During my time we were obliged to fire at them several times.

There was a curious inconsistency in their conduct, as one day they would appear good humoured and friendly, and allow individuals of our settlement to pass through extended lines of them, and probably on the following day throw their spears at any individual they could surprise by stealing upon him. They never came near us without their spears and waddies, but sometimes they would leave their spears concealed behind a tree, or in possession of boys, who would run with them on the first signal; they would then approach within fifty or sixty paces, extend their arms, throw their waddies to the rear, in token of amity, and then by signs oblige all who approached them from our side to extend their arms also, and turn round, to show they had no weapon concealed. When satisfied, they would enter into a palaver, and two or three of the most daring would advance in front of the others, which latter would remain ready to support them in case of emergency. . . I have not space to relate any of their daring and cunning acts of aggression; but we had one savage as a prisoner for several weeks, from whom I learnt a great deal of their character, and the following circumstance caused me to conjecture the reason of their being so suspicious of strangers.

In one of my interviews with a tribe of the aborigines who had approached to within half-a-mile of the fort, I observed they appeared more familiar than usual. Having previously prepared a medal attached to a piece of scarlet tape, I expressed a wish to hang it round the neck of a fine young man, who bore a feather in his hair, and appeared to have some authority. This man remained at... a distance, took hold of his wrists, and appeared as if struggling to escape from an enemy; he then pointed his hand towards his neck, looked upwards to a tree, shook his head significantly (evidently in allusion to being hung), and avoided coming nigh enough to receive the proffered gift. This led me to imagine that the island had been visited by strangers, and the natives forced away by them as slaves, in corroboration of which I add... other circumstances which came under my notice: The first is, that the Malay fishermen, from Macassar, are forbidden to go near Melville Island (which they call 'Amba', signifying a slave), alleging an enmity with the Malays. It is infested by pirates—probably slavers. The second circumstance relates to a lad, who had been taken from a native tribe in 1825, and detained at the settlement three or four days, when he escaped. This lad was the colour of a Malay, and possessed of their features, whence it is probable he was taken when a child from some Malay slave-ship, and reared among the Melville Islanders.

During the four years this island was occupied, only two aboriginal females were seen, and at a distance. They were both old and ugly, and their only garment was a short, narrow strip of plaited grass. We frequently saw boys who were plump, good-looking, and with a remarkable expression of sharpness in their eyes. Their weapons are spears and waddies, their spears are from ten to twelve feet long, made of heavy wood, and very sharp-pointed; some are plain, others barbed; some have a single row of barbs, others a double row, from twelve to fifteen in number; they may weigh three pounds, and are thrown from the hand (without any artificial lever as at Port Jackson) with great precision, to a distance of fifty or sixty yards. Their waddies are used as weapons of attack, as well as for killing wild animals. They are twenty-two inches long, one and a half in diameter, pointed sharp at one end, and weighing about two pounds; they are not round and smooth, but have sixteen equal sides, with rude carving at the handle, to ensure their being held firm in the hand. Their canoes, water buckets, and baskets are made of bark, neatly sewn with strips of split cane.

The natives of Melville and Bathurst Islands are divided into tribes of from thirty to fifty persons each. I never saw above thirty-five or forty men together, although some individuals have reported having seen a hundred in the forest: the noise they make, and their jumping from tree to tree make them often appear more numerous than they really are. They lead a wandering life, though I think each tribe confines itself to a limited district. In 1824-5 a tribe of daring athletic men kept constantly in the neighbourhood of Fort Dundas. In the beginning of 1826 a strange tribe visited the settlement, and they were generally slightly made men. During the dry season they disperse themselves a great deal on hunting excursions, and burnt the grass on the forest ground for that purpose from April to September. When they move, their women and children accompany them, as female voices were frequently heard at a distance at night coming from their encampments.

The food of these people consists of kangaroo, opossum, bandicoot, iguanas, and lizards during the dry months; fish, turtle, crab, and other shell-fish, during the wet months. Their vegetables are the cabbage palm and fruit of the sago palm. They eat their meals just warmed through on a wood fire, and the seed of the sago palm* is made into a mash. Amongst those natives whom we encountered I never saw any deformed or having the appearance of disease or old age; probably such were left with the women, and only the able warriors came near us. There was one powerful, determined looking fellow frequently seen who had lost a hand, and threw his spear by resting it on his maimed arm and taking an aim. [33]

---

*   Cycad

9

PIRATES

A chain of small islands stretches east from Timor through azure waters, visited nowadays by just a few international yachtsmen and semi-regular small planes and inter-island ferries from Surabaya, Ambon, or Kupang. The islands are mostly limestone, with occasional small karst formations draped in lush greenery. Coconut palms fringe the coasts, and huge *Callophyllum* trees throw their shade over the snow-white sand of the coral beaches. Rain is a regular afternoon event and dramatic lightning shows erupt from cumulonimbus thunderheads that hover above the seas. The sun rises and sets in spectacular colour most days. This region is above the cyclone belt that whips Australia in the south, so its normally balmy climate stands in contrast to that of its southern neighbour. There are few surf beaches, as most of the islands are protected by ancient coral reefs, so few tourists ever come this way.

These islands are about as remote as you can get in Indonesia. They fall into two groups known as the Serwatti and the Tanimbar Islands, and their names are unfamiliar to outsiders: Palau Maselar, Pulau Babar, Pulau Jamdena (known as Timor Laut), Palau Delu,

Palau Leti, and others. Close your eyes and think of a tropical island paradise, and images of these unknown islands may appear.

During the colonial times, the Dutch government mostly ignored the islands. They were 'possessions,' too remote for all but the most ardent missionaries and too far from Java to effectively wield the rod of Dutch Law. There is a story that Babar Island used to have valuable nutmeg trees growing wild in the forest. Apparently, the Dutch destroyed them because the nuts were too far away to harvest, and if they couldn't have them, then no one else was going to either [140]. The islands' small populations had a simple economic system based on market centres on Pulau Leti, which brought in some goods. However, they mostly kept themselves alive through fishing, small plot farming, or slash and burn agriculture maintaining close animist and cultural ties between themselves. Today, the islanders are mostly Catholic, and their villages cluster around a central church, yet traditional customs survive in elaborate drum dances and ancestor worship.

In the eighteenth and nineteenth centuries, unwelcome visitors targeted these islands. Slavers would round up the unwary and cart them off to the great slave markets in Batavia. As the islands were outside the influence of law and order, such as it was, some of the islanders also became lawless. Their response to slavery and the savagery of the outside world was in kind. Some became pirates and accepted visits from outsiders on their terms only—with violence, murder, and theft.

The Serwatti and Tanimbar Islands lie in an arc several days sail north of Fort Dundas. Timor, which lies northwest from Melville Island and Kupang (aka Koepang and Coepang), on the far west end of Timor, is about twice as far as the Tanimbar group. A helmsman would not steer to the Tanimbar Islands by accident—the compass would need to turn about 80°N from the bearing for Kupang.

The dangers of visiting Babar and other islands because of piracy were well known among sailors at the time. When Captain Samuel Johns and his nine crewmen sailed the *Lady Nelson* northwards to the Tanimbar Islands, rather than westwards to Timor, they must have done so deliberately and known they were taking a risk. However, despite the fact that he was disobeying his orders, in spirit, if not actually on paper, Johns decided on the more dangerous destination. Miller had told him to

> *"... go to the islands to purchase whatever stock he could get, he having stated that sheep, goats and buffalo were easier procurable there than pigs, and to return as soon as possible."*[89]

Johns had recently returned from Kupang only a few weeks previously when he took the commissariat officer, George Miller, from Fort Dundas to Timor to purchase livestock. Miller had bought thirty small, weedy pigs and some other produce. Whilst in the port, they ran into Captain Barns who was also heading for Fort Dundas in command of the *Stedcombe*.

Kupang and Fort Dundas were only some six hundred kilometres apart, but the adverse winds of the wet season ensured the return leg took fourteen days, and Johns and Miller were away for five weeks. When they got home, they were shocked to see several of their community already weakening from the effects of scurvy.

Commandant Barlow immediately ordered Johns to turn the *Lady Nelson* round and return to Kupang as a matter of urgency. To make double sure, when the *Stedcombe* arrived in Port Cockburn four days later, Barlow chartered it as well, agreeing with Barns that he would pay twenty-five Spanish dollars each for buffaloes landed alive at Fort Dundas. The *Stedcombe*, under the command of the Chief Mate Bastell, headed out of Apsley Strait on 19 February 1825 with orders to return to Kupang and be back at Fort Dundas within five weeks. But Bastell *also* chose to head north to the closer islands. By May, Barlow was worried:

> *"Barns' schooner (the Stedcombe) left this port four days after Johns' departure [in the Lady Nelson], in charge of his Chief Mate,*

101

*neither have returned since. I fear they either have been wrecked or
fallen into the hands of the Malay Pirates."* [13]

So, even though Captain Johns and First Mate Bastell were warned
to keep clear of the Tanimbar Island area because it was 'infested
with pirates who were very daring and very cruel,' [80] the warnings
were ignored, and both ships headed northwards immediately. Why
they did this is a matter of conjecture. They were certainly in a hurry,
and the islands to the north may have been an easier run. Whatever
the reason, both ships sailed to their doom.

The *Lady Nelson* went first to Pulau Leti, but the crew seems to
have been lured east to the remote coast of Babar Island with promises
of supplies of stock, only to be overrun by pirates. If this was the
case, it was a well-planned and organised criminal operation. The
ship's crew were murdered, and she was stripped, burned, and sunk.

The *Stedcombe* met the same fate soon after, some ninety kilometres
farther east, at an island then known as *Timor Laut,* but today called
Pulau Jamdena. The coincidence is remarkable, as both ships were
on emergency supply runs for the only British settlement in the area,
and both captains disobeyed orders to head there in the first place.
It is probable that the people of each island knew of the other's
activities. The late historian, Peter Spillett suggested the *Stedcombe*
was only attacked because of the lack of official response to the
murders of the *Lady Nelson* crew, despite the short time interval
between the two events.

A Dutch Brig of War, the *Dourga* visited Tepa on Babar Island
several months later. Its commander, Lieutenant Kolff reported that
he found it nearly deserted—the villagers had headed for the hills.
Kolff said he was convinced a crime had been committed and in
discussion with the head men of Tepa he:

*"...succeeded in gaining some of the particulars concerning it from
a few of the natives. It appeared that some months previous to my visit,*

an English trading brig, manned with ten European seamen, which had been bartering muskets and ammunition for tortoiseshell and cattle among the islands to the eastward of Timor anchored off Aloetor, the capital of the tribe inhabiting the east side of Baba, and the commander, supposing the people to be as trustworthy as those of the other islands, sent half his crew ashore in the boat to obtain water, at a time when a large number of natives were on board the brig carrying on a trade. While the boat was away, the natives, for some unknown reason, attacked the commander and the four remaining seamen and, although only with their knives, succeeded in killing them, which fate also befell the boat's crew on their return on board. The brig was then run ashore, plundered and burnt. The greater part of her cargo, consisting of arms, tortoiseshell and cattle, together with her sails and rigging, which had been divided among the captors, were still in their possession." [77]

The next year in Sydney, a ship called *The Faith* arrived with news that the hull of the *Lady Nelson* was still to be seen at Babar Island with her name painted on the stern. Brief reports of the fate of the *Lady Nelson* appeared in the Gazette over the next few months:

"By the arrival of the Faith, we learn, that the Lady Nelson had been despatched from Melville Island for fresh provisions to some of the islands in the neighbourhood of Timor, with instructions to avoid an island named Babba [Babar], where they would be in great danger of her being cut off. This advice, however, unfortunately was not adhered to, but whether it was so by accident or design, we have not ascertained; the result is certain. Every soul on board, we regret to state, was cruelly massacred, and the hull of the vessel was seen some time after with the name painted on her stern." [133]

Cattle die, wood, ropes, and riggings rot away, but if the villagers plundered the *Lady Nelson* as the story went, then *something* must remain. These were Peter Spillett's thoughts, and he had the opportunity

103

to follow them up in 1981, when he convinced the skipper of *La Baleine*, a competitor in the Darwin to Ambon yacht race, to participate in an expedition looking for any relics of the ships on the return journey after the race.

After sailing through difficult winds and following a trail of rumours and half remembered stories, Spillett finally reached the village of Tutuwawang on the eastern coast of Babar Island. There in the garden of an old man's house, where it had lain for one hundred and sixty-five years, was the carronade from the *Lady Nelson* herself. You can imagine Spillett's excitement at this discovery. Carronades are small guns, which were mounted on ships but portable enough to be taken ashore if necessary. This one was just over a metre long, with a stubby breach. It was marked with a broad arrow and the numbers 6-1-7. Spillett asked the village head man to write down the story, as he knew it, and he later managed a loose translation. Bapak Brony Erbably wrote:

> *"Whist the ship rode at anchor, a woman relieved herself on the beach. The crew abused her. She called to her countrymen to come and kill those on board. Whereupon the ship was pushed ashore. The person who was the leader at that time was Moses Erbably."* [130]

Was the ship's destruction revenge for a crime or cruel piracy? We'll never know for sure, but it was a tragedy for nine seamen and their captain, and a sad end to a plucky little ship which had played an important role in the settlement of New Holland. The *Lady Nelson's* twenty-four year Australian career of service before she was sent to Fort Dundas is well known, and Tasmanians are particularly well aware of her and her importance in their history. Plying the island state's waters is a modern replica built to honour her.

The second ship lost that month in 1825 is much less well known. The *Stedcombe* had no glorious past to revere, made no major discoveries,

104

nor helped in any other new colonisation attempts. But she had one thing the *Lady Nelson* unfortunately didn't have: *survivors*!

Figure 11 The replica Lady Nelson in Tasmania (by courtesy ladynelson.org.au)

The *Stedcombe* had been sold by a Mr Brookes to members of the East India Trade Committee, Palmer, Wilson & Co, who had

> "...united in the purchase of a vessel which they are sending out with a cargo under the superintendence of Captain Barns, for the purpose of opening a trade with the natives of the north coast of New Holland, and with other people frequenting that coast or about the situation of the proposed settlement." [78]

She was heartily welcomed in Port Cockburn. Commandant Barlow was desperately worried about the scurvy outbreak and the *Lady Nelson*, which had departed only four days previously, was too small to bring back the amount of provisions needed by the weakening community. Barns was welcomed as well—Barlow loaned him some of the best land near the jetty to set up his business, and he set to

105

work supervising the building of his house and a store. Thus occupied, he was too busy to go anywhere, so he sent First Mate Bastell in his place with orders to return within five weeks bringing live buffalo.

Lieutenant Kolff, in the *Dourga*, had left Babar Island after he had heard the story about the *Lady Nelson* and continued eastwards, stopping at many of the Tanimbar Islands, talking with the inhabitants and asking about trading vessels who may have visited. He was, therefore, the first to hear the gossip about the *Stedcombe*. On the small island of Larrat, which lies adjacent to the largest of the Tanimbar group, Palau Jamdena, he was told of a British vessel that had been recently carrying 'on a smuggling trade.' The captain had bartered with the islanders to trade weapons for stock and had taken half his crew of ten to the shore:

> *"In the meantime the natives considered this to be a fine opportunity to overpower those who remained on board, and gain possession of the vessel. They, therefore, boarded her unexpectedly in great numbers and murdered the people in her, whilst at the same time those on shore were made away with, with the exception of two boys, who owed their preservation to the interposition of the women. After this crime had been committed they hauled the brig on shore, stripped her of all that they could carry away, and burned her. The plundered goods were shared among the inhabitants, and part of them sold to traders who visited them, the remainder being kept, and now perhaps, serving as finery for the inhabitants of the east coast of Timor Laut. One of the village chiefs stated to me that he had seen the chain cable of the brig hanging around the village, and that two carronades which had belonged to her lay there on the ground, the natives not having yet mustered sufficient courage to fire them off."* [77]

Lieutenant Kolff was not in a position to do anything with the information—the captive boys were British and, in his opinion, smugglers, so he sailed away north towards the Banda Islands to continue his work, leaving them to their fate. However, when he returned later in the year to another neighbouring island, Pulau Vordate, he spoke with a chief who had seen two European boys on Timor Laut and was sure he could rescue them on the payment of a substantial ransom. However, at that time of year, landing at the village of Laoura (Lauran), where the boys were supposed to be, was impossible:

> *"… at the present time, when the sea breaks upon the shore in a terrible manner, such an expedition was not to be thought of for a moment."*

Kolff again left them behind.

Rumours ran rife, but those in Fort Dundas heard nothing of the *Stedcombe* until Captain Samuel Dowsett of the *Mermaid* arrived in late September 1826 with a cargo of buffalo from Kupang. Campbell recorded the news Dowsett related:

> *"Monsieur Becharde, a French merchant, residing at Coepang, told him that a small vessel from Melville Island had been taken by the Malays near the island of Tinomber or Tinaniver, about six months back; that the crew excepting one small boy had been massacred; that this boy had been afterwards ransomed by the Dutch government for two muskets and was carried to Batavia. This information came to Coepang by a Dutch ship of war which touched there; and Mr Becharde had learned the same account at Java. The schooner had a boy on board when she sailed from this island and the Lady Nelson had none."* [33]

Nothing more of the boy or the *Stedcombe* came to light for a number of years. Then in 1834, the *Charles Eaton* was wrecked on a reef in the Torres Straits. There were many lives lost, but one of the ship's boats escaped the sinking ship. The five men lucky enough to be on board set sail directly for Kupang, and, after two weeks westwards travel, they reached the island of Timor Laut and called in at the village of Olitit. This was nearly fatal as they were immediately attacked by the villagers, but with the intervention of the village chiefs, managed to survive, recuperate

,and wait for rescue. Whilst there, they heard stories of other Europeans in a neighbouring and enemy village, Laoura, who were 'survivors of a shipwreck' some seven years earlier, and, although one of them had since died, the other had turned native and did not want to leave the island.

The *Charles Eaton* survivors waited thirteen months for their rescue by a trading prahu from Amboyna, [86] and thus the news of the boy was delayed further. Finally, on 6 December 1835, they arrived in Batavia and made a sworn joint deposition of their story. This reached England in June 1836, eleven years after the *Stedcombe* had gone missing. Nothing more was heard of the boy until a Dutch captain named Volshawn, master of a small trading vessel, actually saw an Englishman on the island of Timor Laut when he visited it in February or March 1838. He discovered that he was a captive at Laoura village, and he had also seen objects there, which had been taken from the *Stedcombe*. However, because Volshawn had had a native crew, he made no attempt to rescue him.

Meanwhile the British were establishing Victoria Settlement in Port Essington using *HMS Alligator, HMS Britomart*, and a transport vessel *Orontes**. Captain Gordon Bremer, despite his failure at choosing a poor site for Fort Dundas, had again been called in to found a new settlement. After a few weeks, he left Captain John MacArthur as its commandant. Whilst Bremer was still there, a private ship, the *Essington*, which had previously been named the *Isabella,* arrived under the command of Captain Thomas Watson.

Watson had met Volshawn at Kupang and brought news of the captive to Victoria Settlement. Bremer immediately sent the *Britomart*, under Lieutenant Owen Stanley, to the islands but he failed to find any Europeans, though he did leave a letter at the village, which the chief would produce later, along with some scraps of paper and notes written by the *Charles Eaton* crew.

Convinced that the boy must have been hidden, Bremer determined to try to rescue him himself when he could quit Port Essington.

---

* The *Orontes* hit a reef soon after she left the new settlement and quickly sank.

However, in the meantime, he chartered the *Essington* to import livestock and other foods, and encouraged Captain Watson to arrange a rescue for his countryman whilst he was in the area.

Watson managed to find the now thirty-one year old 'boy,' a shoemaker's son from London named Joseph Forbes, and bring him back to English civilisation.

Captain Watson recorded meeting Forbes in his log:

"The appearance of this Englishman at the time we received him on board, was in the highest degree, remarkable, and such as was calculated to draw forth, the strongest sympathies from the bosom of any human being, whose composition was not entirely void of compassionate feelings. He appeared, as far as one can judge from his looks, as well as from the length of time he must have been upon the island, to be about 26 years of age; of a remarkably fair complexion, notwithstanding the effects of a tropical climate. There was also a delicacy of frame about him, seldom to be met with in a person of his years. His hair, which was of a lightest yellow colour, had been allowed to grow long, and was triced up after the native custom with a comb made of Bamboo. The length of the hair was from 18 to 20 inches, and its texture very much resembled the finest silk in its raw state. His only garments were a sort of waist coat, without sleeves, and a blue and white dungaree girdle round his loins. There was a peculiar vacancy in his countenance, which I am at a loss to describe, but I can compare it to nothing more aptly than to that aspect, observable in deaf and dumb people, besides there was an expression of agony in his, which from long continued suffering no doubt, had become habitual. His body was much emaciated and covered with numberless scars, the evidence of the savage tortures he had endured; and his legs were studded with ulcers, and the sinews about his knee joints were so much contracted, as to prevent him extending his legs, and consequently, rendering him unable to walk. His ears had been perforated after the custom of the natives, and the hole in the lobe of each, is large enough to admit of his wearing a piece of Bamboo, at least one inch in diameter;

indeed, he did wear such a piece at the time he was brought off. As might have been expected from having been on the island 16 years, he had almost forgotten his native language." [141]

When he reached Sydney, the story of the rescue held a lot of public interest. *The Colonist* reported on 27 July 1839:

"Rescue of a British Subject from the Savages of Timor Laut
CAPTAIN WATSON has favoured us with the following brief outline of his rescue of Joseph Forbes, from the natives of the Island of Timor Laut: Captain Watson had heard that Forbes was on the island, and that the Britomart had been there, but was unsuccessful in getting the boy. When Captain Watson arrived off the island he was determined, if possible, to bring him away. He had not been off the island long, before the Essington was surrounded by eleven armed canoes for the purpose of attack. The chief wished Captain Watson to go in and anchor, which he refused, but showed him that he was ready for defence in case of any outrage on their part. The chief, thinking he could entrap him, made signs of friendship and Captain Watson allowed him and his crew to come on board.

The chief then said that a white man was on shore, and wished the Captain to go and fetch him off, which was refused. Captain Watson then laid out an immense quantity of merchandise, which he said he would give for the white man, and desired the chief to send his canoe ashore to fetch him stating, however, that he would retain him on board till the white man came, and also, that if he was not immediately brought, he would either hang or shoot the chief; and he had a rope prepared for the purpose, as also a gun. This manoeuvre had the desired effect on the chief, who immediately despatched his canoe to the shore. For three days and nights Captain Watson was compelled to cruise off the island, the natives still refusing to bring off Forbes. Towards the close of the third day they brought off the boy, but would not put him on board, until Captain Watson placed the rope round the chief's neck, when they came alongside-and as the crew of the Essington were hoisting Forbes up the side of the vessel, the chief jumped overboard into his canoe.

Captain Watson made the chief come on board again, and told him that although he had deceived, and wished to entrap him, yet he would show that the white men were as good as their words, and not only gave the chief the promised wares, but also distributed some to each of the other ten canoes. This line of conduct had a very good effect on the natives, who, after receiving the goods, expressed great joy, and as they were leaving, kept up a constant cheer.

Forbes at first appeared in a savage state… The sinews of his legs are much contracted, and he has a great number of ulcers and sores all over his legs and body. Fortunately for Forbes, Captain Watson had a surgeon on board the Essington, who immediately put him under a course of medicine, which, without doubt, saved his life-for, from the emaciated state in which he was received on board, it was impossible, without medical aid, that he could have survived much longer. We trust that the Government will do something for the unfortunate fellow." [42]

The Sydney Gazette reported the arrival of Watson and Forbes in Sydney on Saturday 20 July 1839:

"TORRES' Strait The Essington, schooner, Captain Watson, arrived on Thursday night, brings with him a young man named Joseph Forbes, picked up by Captain Watson at Laoura, Timor Laut, in Torres' Straits, on the 1st of April last. Forbes, it appears, is the only survivor of the crew of the schooner Stedcombe of London, which was forcibly taken possession of, and ultimately destroyed and the crew massacred by the savages at Timor Laut, in 1822."*

---

* Joseph Forbes was the ship's cabin boy. He was born in Deptford in Kent, England in 1806 or 1807.

But what had happened? How had Forbes survived? He took several weeks to reacquaint himself with the English language, and as his skills improved, his story caught the imagination of the nation:

First Mate Bastell had brought the Stedcombe into the bay at night and had moored in calm water to await daylight. Early in the next morning, they had rowed the ship's boat to the shore carrying old muskets, hatchets, and other items to trade for food, livestock, and tortoiseshell with the islanders. The seventeen-year-old Joseph Forbes and another boy, John Edwards, were left on the ship with the steward to prepare lunch for the crew and attend to their normal duties.

About mid-day, Forbes checked the beach through the telescope in order to tell the steward if the crew were returning for their lunch. He was in time to see dreadful events unfold on the beach. As Forbes watched, he saw that the islanders were holding the crew as prisoners. Suddenly, they started killing Forbes's companions with knives and clubs, cutting off their heads. His older brother, also a member of the crew, was slain as young Joseph watched.

Horrified, Forbes tried to rouse the steward, who at first refused to believe him, and only came on deck after Forbes and Edwards had slipped the cable and set the ship adrift, but by then, canoes were already heading their way. The three tried to set a sail, but were quickly overrun and the ship was boarded. Terrified, Forbes and Edwards quickly scaled the rigging. The steward was surrounded, and one of the islanders immediately cut his head off with an axe he found on deck [141]*.

Then, a small bow anchor was dropped and the pirates began to plunder the ship, taunting the boys in the rigging, shooting arrows at them, and cajoling them to come down. Eventually, in the evening, the village chief convinced them that they would not be harmed, and still fearing the worst, they descended into captivity:

---

* An alternative account from the Sydney Gazette (1839) is that the islander "dashed his brains out with a bit of handspike and threw the body overboard"

"The savages immediately stripped them, put them into the canoes and took them ashore. On their arrival the boys found that the savages had arranged the headless bodies of their murdered companions in a line on the beach, over which they were compelled to walk, Forbes recognising the remains of his brother, one of the crew, in the third body on which he had to tread. On the following day the bodies were thrown into the bay. The heads were tied together and hung upon a tree, in the centre of the village, round which the savages danced for three successive days and nights. Subsequently when decomposition had advanced to such a degree as to become offensive, the heads were taken down and placed... near the beach, where they remained until buried by the boy Forbes, without the knowledge of the savages, about six years afterwards.

On the day succeeding that on which the massacre took place the savages ransacked the vessel, and after taking everything out of her to which they took a fancy, they hauled her up on the beach and set fire to her." [135]

The boys entered lives of slavery. They were used as farm labourers, planting coconuts, plantains, yams, melons, and tobacco in the village fields by day, and then sent out in tiny canoes to catch fish by night. They were fed a subsistence diet, but were not treated well and would be 'knocked down' if they didn't do what they were told immediately. Their lives improved, as they learned the local language and understood what they had to do, and John Edwards even had a son with a local woman named Ampokyenan, whom they named Mparunaman. His descendants can still be identified seven generations later.

Edwards died after about seven years through 'the effects of exposure to the sun, and the ill treatment of the savages' [135]. His body was hung in a tree in a woven basket until it rotted away, and Forbes collected his bones as they fell to the ground and buried them under the tree, as he continued to live his life of slavery in the village:

113

> *"The savages cut his ears and suspended from them large silver ear rings, nearly half around each in weight. His teeth were filed to the gums, his arms burnt, and the back of his right hand tattooed. Whenever a vessel hove in sight he was bound hand and foot and carried into the interior until the vessel had gone."* [135]

Forbes was 'carried' because he couldn't walk properly. Some sources say that he had a 'disease of the feet,' another says that his tendons had become short because of the many hours he'd been forced to sit in cramped fishing canoes and he could no longer straighten them, and yet another that his feet were damaged from walking on hot sand.

> *"Nor does the Catalogue of this poor fellow's misfortunes end here, for he was found to have been injured in the Genitals, and on being questioned about it, he said it was caused by the bite of the Native Wild Pig."* [140]

Forbes also told of at least four other ships which had been plundered by the pirates and that he'd heard of other European slaves kept on the adjacent islands, including two from the *Lady Nelson*. He told of a Chinese junk that the pirates had boarded. They had murdered the crew and plundered anything of value, then burnt the ship. Then, he said, there was a schooner manned with black men who were robbed then set free, and about three years previously, the pirates had taken a Dutch ship and murdered its crew. As a reprisal the Dutch government had raised the village to the ground with artillery and fire, killing the elderly occupants of some of the houses who were too feeble to flee the fire. [135]

Captain Watson delivered Forbes to Sydney, and Captain Bremer, who arrived from Port Essington on *HMS Alligator* at about the same time, organised hospital treatment for him. He was a celebrity for a while and there was a public collection to help him, ironically started by the original owner of the *Stedcombe*, Mr Brookes, who opened the subscription with five pounds.

114

In 1840, Watson wrote to the *London Times* asking for the editor's help in tracking down any old friends or relatives, and Forbes travelled to England to meet them on the proceeds of the subscription. He returned to Australia a few years later as a seaman, and worked on a trading vessel that ran between Sydney and Melbourne from 1854 until 1857, and then as a ship keeper on a Bethel Ship*. Forbes retired to Williamstown, Victoria where he died in 1877.

Forbes wasn't forgotten. Captain C Pasco, who had been a lieutenant on board the *Britomart* in 1838, presented a paper telling the history of Forbes's enslavement and rescue to the newly formed Historical Society of Australia in 1886. His story was later dramatized, with some poetic licence, in *In the Clutches of Black Pirates* by *The Argus*, in 1838.

Just over a hundred years later, the same paper published the following letter:

"THE BETHEL SHIP

Sir,—May I add to Mr. A. W. Greig's paragraph on 'The Bethel Ship,' as published in last Saturday's 'Bygone Days' column. In addition to the chaplain and his family, there was a ship keeper named Joe Forbes, residing on the Seaman's Bethel Ship, and he had a rather curious history. Forbes came out from London as a lad of 17 in the brig Stedcombe in 1823, and in 1826 this vessel was dispatched from the first settlement in North Australia (Melville Island) by the commandant to procure buffaloes and provisions for the garrison. Nothing more was heard of the vessel and it was presumed that she had been wrecked.

In April 1839, Captain Watson, of the schooner Essington, while engaged in a private trading venture among the islands to the north of Australia, heard from a Dutch vessel that there was a European captive at Timor Laut. He accordingly approached the island, and by strategy

---

* 'Bethel ships' were floating chapels made from old unseaworthy ships that were moored at piers.

secured possession of the captive. It seems the Stedcombe visited the island to trade, but imprudently anchored, and the natives boarded the ship, overpowering and murdering the crew, with the exception of Joe Forbes, whom they kept as a slave. His hair had been allowed to grow, and he was in a completely naked and wretched condition when rescued.

Forbes was taken to Sydney, and eventually returned to London. He again returned to Australia as a seaman, trading between Melbourne and Sydney until 1857, when he became ship keeper of the Seaman's Bethel at Melbourne. When wharf accommodation was provided at Sandridge the Bethel was erected on shore and Joe's occupation was gone. He lived until 1877, dying at the age of 71.

Yours &c
EM Christie, Melbourne" [6]

Finally, on 25 June 1959, *The Age* wrote the story of 'Jimmy' Forbes in an article titled *The Pirates of Baba Island* in a section called *The World's Strangest Stories*:

"In the middle years of last century, a well-known character at Williamstown was a little, bent-up man who earned a living of sorts fishing in the Bay. He was known as Jimmy Forbes.

Whence he came, how old he was, none knew, and Jimmy would not, or could not, tell.

He had a peculiar, shuffling walk, as though his knee joints were dried out. His English was halting, stilted. But he spoke Malay fluently..." [1]

Forbes is remembered in a short street named after him in the Darwin suburb of Alawa. Forbes Street intersects with Stedcombe Street, named after his ship, and around the corner lies Watson Street, which honours his rescuer.

10

THE SUCCESS AND THE FAILURE

It is easy to conclude that Fort Dundas failed as a settlement and so too its sister, Fort Wellington, a day's sail to the east. The settlements were certainly unsuccessful commercially, as both were rarely visited by traders or Macassans, and those that came found that nothing was produced of economic importance in the communities anyway. They were also unsuccessful physically because of the difficulty in maintaining a healthy population of more than a hundred people, with little knowledge about farming in the tropical climate, extremely poor supply lines, and the length of time it took for communication with the outside world.

Despite this, one major objective was achieved, well, because the English could now demonstrate their claim to the north coast of the continent to the other European powers who may have been interested. The boundaries of New South Wales were redrawn from longitude 135°E westwards to longitude 129°E. Then, when the Swan River Colony was established in 1832, Britain claimed the remainder of the continent. These occupations legitimised the English claim in the eyes of the international community, if not the local Aboriginal tribes. The border between Western Australia and the Northern Territory and South Australia still remains at 129°E.

Ironically, the establishment of 'provenance' by settling the north may have been unnecessary. Peter Spillett, who remarkably taught himself Dutch and travelled to Holland to read for himself the records of their intentions in the area, could find no evidence of a Dutch desire to settle northern Australia. In 1824, Phillip Parker King's surveys were yet to be published, and as Spillett said, 'Who plans a settlement on a foreign shore without surveys?' He concluded that the Dutch never had any intention of settling North Australia.

In fact, both the Dutch and French had both come and gone in earlier times. The former had come looking for business in a new country with which to trade, but they found what they thought was 'a barren wasteland, inhabited by people who had no possessions of value for exchange.'[58] The French who visited were undertaking poorly funded scientific explorations from a country, which was still crippled from the long lasting effects of the Napoleonic Wars, so there was never any intention to make a settlement by them either.

Forrest[57] argues that for many years after 1705, the Tiwi Islands, Melville and Bathurst, and their people, were the best known parts of Australia to outsiders. Moreover, even though the Dutch may have named the continent *Nova Hollandia* and knew more than any other country about its north coast through several centuries of exploration, they were, at the very least, ambivalent about the British taking it on. Forrest points out that this was fundamental to Australian history because, based on this knowledge, the Dutch had no interest in the continent and left it to others to claim her.

Or at least, so it seemed. De La Rue[49] connects the establishment of Fort Dundas and Fort Wellington to a similar settlement made by the Dutch, named Merkus-oord on Triton Bay in western New Guinea, and the fort they built there called Fort De Bus, in 1828. With this occupation, the Dutch had extended their own provenance in the archipelago eastwards to longitude 141°E. This was political posturing. Both countries had signed a treaty, known as the London Treaty, to resolve any trade and territorial conflicts in 1824, but nevertheless, both became involved in manoeuvres designed to exclude the other from territory they saw as important to their country's interests, claiming their actions were commercial in intent. Like those in North Australia, the Dutch settlements struggled with disease and raids from local people, and their much weakened survivors were eventually repatriated in 1836.

The difficulties faced by the small settlements proved insurmountable in the short term. Fort Dundas lasted a little over four years, hardly any time at all, before it was deserted and left to the white ants. Several factors helped its demise: the incompetence of the commandants and their lack of knowledge of the islands; the location of the fort; the health and disease challenges they experienced; and the Tiwi, who kept them virtually besieged behind their timber walled fort. Fort Wellington lasted just two years for similar reasons.

A number of maladies worked their way through the settlers during the four years of its operation, and many of the deaths that occurred can be attributed to them. The doctors' *Return of the Sick* was a register of ailments, who suffered them, and what treatment they received. Campbell reported to the Geographical Society in 1834 that he could:

"... perfectly recollect the prevailing diseases..., as well as many of the deaths. The prevailing diseases were: intermittent, acute, and typhus fevers, constipation of the bowels, vertigo (frequent), dysentery, diarrhoea, rheumatism, scurvy, and nectalopia* (sic); the latter disease was very common. The cases of typhus and acute fever appeared at the beginning of the wet season; and when the winds were variable during that period, many were suddenly seized with sickness, violent griping and delirium. We could not account for the prevalence of nectalopia, or, as it is sometimes called, moon-blindness. Salt meat

---

*   *Nyctalopia* or night blindness can be linked to a deficiency in vitamin A.

was certainly generally issued 'to every person, but they had, besides, a wholesome proportion of flour, rice or bread, with vinegar, tea, sugar, salt, a small quantity of vegetables; nor were the settlers exposed to any extraordinary glare from sand or water and many who had this complaint used very little of their salt meat. Even when fresh meat was issued, this disease prevailed to a considerable extent."

Scurvy is a disease that has killed more sailors than storms, shipwrecks, combat, and all other diseases combined—more than two million sailors died of it during the Age of Sail.[23] It afflicts people anywhere if they have insufficient access to fresh vegetables or fruits and the vitamin C they contain. It was seen in towns sieged during wars, in prisons, and in countries enduring famines. It has even occurred in remote cattle or mining camps in Australia. On a diet of salt port, biscuits, and grog it takes only a matter of six weeks or so for the first symptoms to appear. Scurvy is a disintegration of the body's connective tissue, which leads to bleeding gums, teeth falling out, foul smelling breath, anaemia, lethargy, and weakness. Long healed broken bones can separate once more, and it leads to a slow death if untreated.

As previously described, the Fort Dundas doctors were 'assistant surgeons' who probably knew little about tropical diseases, but scurvy, one of the diseases they dealt with most often, was not a *tropical* disease at all. Doctors at the time knew that limes and oranges were a proven remedy for scurvy. Thirty-six years earlier, when the First Fleet victualed in Rio de Janeiro during its two hundred and fifty day journey to Botany Bay, the crew and convicts were fed 'great numbers of oranges... (to) put them in a condition to resist the attacks of scurvy.'[41] In other settlements around the colony, lime juice had been issued routinely to military and prisoners alike. For example, Assistant Surgeon Fenton of the 48th Regiment of Foot based at the Port Macquarie settlement, used it to 'overcome the slow healing of wounds, cuts and scratches' in 1823.'[118]

The initial settlers at Fort Dundas had been provided with an amount of lime juice when they first occupied the island. We know this because, on 25 May 1825, Assistant Surgeon Turner wrote to Commandant Barlow saying that the original supply of lime juice was exhausted and as it 'is most valuable in this colony, may I beg we may be supplied with it whenever an opportunity occurs.' However, the Fort Dundas commandants and the assistant surgeons failed to ensure lime juice was given the respect it deserved when victualing their community. Even in a time when the English were getting to be called 'Limeys' because of their medicinal use of limes, they continued to blame the disease on the climate. In the end, lives were only saved by chance or by sending sick people back to Sydney.

No one ever wondered how the Tiwi could be so healthy or, perhaps, if they did, they assumed it was a matter of racial disposition. No one seems to have compared the settlers' salt-meat diet to that of the locals. Vitamin C is everywhere in the Top End bush if one is willing to eat native fruits. The green plum or billy goat plum, *Terminalia ferdinandiana*, is a tree that grows in the forest in which Fort Dundas was situated. It bears a small green fruit that contains sixty times the Vitamin C content of oranges. The irony is that some of the men who cleared the forest and later died of scurvy may have cut down green plum trees when they were clearing the land.

By the time the settlement was just eight months old, four convicts had already died of the disease, and many more had spent time in the hospital. But none of the officers ever became scorbutic. The lime juice supply they had was, like the raisins, probably reserved for people of a higher status than the convicts. The tiered meal system the commandants introduced ensured they and the top levels of the society received the little produce that came from the gardens first, whilst the convicts were stuck with salted beef or pork. The commandants were educated men, and they certainly pushed the convicts to grow fresh food, as they connected it to good health, but they were more concerned about the health of the military than the convicts.

121

Campbell was very confused about scurvy:

"With respect to the scurvy, it appeared to me to be an endemic disease arising from some peculiar local cause; with new comers, it might be occasioned by a removal from a cool climate to a heated and damp one. This disease only appeared generally at the settlement of Fort Dundas, shortly after its establishment in 1824. The constant use of salt provisions, without vegetables, hard labour during the wet season, and the excessive heat of that season may have engendered it; and notwithstanding the attention and endeavours of an intelligent and experienced surgeon (Assistant Surgeon Turner) to prevent and afterwards arrest it, the disease made great progress until the end of 1825, or the beginning of 1826. When lime juice was obtained, and vegetables became more plentiful, the disease then subsided. There were, however, several cases of scurvy during 1826, 1827, and 1828, although the utmost caution was taken to guard against it by great attention to cleanliness, use of vegetables, and frequent issues of fresh and preserved meats, pickles and vinegar. [33]

When the first detachment of troops were relieved in 1826 those who replaced them had spirits mixed into grog issued to them every day (the former detachment had no spirits issued); and amongst these very few cases of scurvy appeared, although they lived generally upon salt provisions for the first year, with a very small occasional addition of vegetables, probably once a week."

He mostly blamed the climate for the disease but felt that providing spirits to his men cured scurvy. Luckily, to make it more palatable, the spirits were sometimes drunk in the form of a fruit punch with lime juice, when it was available, and sugar:

"When the settlement was established in Raffles Bay in 1827, on the north coast of New Holland, and in the same parallel with Fort Dundas, at which place no spirits or wine was issued either to the

military or convicts, the scurvy broke out and spread in a rapid and alarming degree, both amongst the soldiers and prisoners.

The site of the settlement and its neighbourhood was dry; the disease occurred during the dry season. The establishment consisted of young healthy men, direct from Sydney, and many of them only a few months from England. The complaint made its appearance among the settlers in six or seven weeks after landing: their diet consisted of a small quantity of salt meat, and occasionally fish (which was caught close to the settlement), with flour, sugar, and tea or coffee. When the malady had attacked and rendered incapable of exertion two thirds of the settlement, spirits, lime juice and sugar made into punch, was issued to all the worst cases, and grog or wine issued to the military. It immediately remitted in virulence, and ultimately nearly or entirely disappeared. I saw all the sufferers myself, having had occasion to go to Raffles Bay; and from my observations and enquiries, I certainly thought that the scurvy there, as well as on Melville Island, was endemic and more dependent on climate and local causes than diet.

Considering the consequences of the climate of Melville Island, during my residence there and that of my predecessor, and knowing the unremitting attention that was paid and measures adopted, in order to preserve health throughout the settlement during my command, I must pronounce it to partake more of the character of an unhealthy than a healthy climate. I should not recommend invalids to go there during any period of the year to be restored to health from any part of the world although from May to September, healthy people may continue in the enjoyment of health with rational care; but from the end of September to May, few can escape some attack or other of illness. The climate, after a year of residence, is extremely debilitating to Europeans; but on the whole, with proper precautions, it does not often engender any fatal complaint. I must however mention one gentleman who suffered much from the climate: this was Mr Miller of the commissariat, who remained in a very debilitated state for a year and more after leaving the island." [33]

The loss of the *Lady Nelson* and the *Stedcombe* came at a disastrous time, as the delay it caused in importing food from Timor resulted not only in several deaths to scurvy, but a debilitated workforce, whose weakness slowed the development of the settlement and crushed the morale of the inhabitants. When Captain Laws visited in 1827, he was scathing at the loss of life, particularly through scurvy, but he was also highly unimpressed by the lack of survival skills the British showed. He suggested the Ceylon Regiment would be better suited to the task of colonisation because:

> *"... by walking half a mile from their camp, (the Ceylon Regiment) would find plenty of the vegetable they had been accustomed to eat all their lives, which vegetables the English soldier (who thinks of no other resource than the Commissariat) looked upon as poison. I had an instance of this in my own servant who, in a quarter of an hour, collected vegetables to make a curry, and therefore to him a dinner."*[79]

Scurvy wasn't always a death sentence—given a boost of vitamin C the men would recover and many did. For example, one of the convicts who arrived on the *Countess of Harcourt* in 1824 was Charles Green, a young bricklayer from Bromley. He fell sick with scurvy in January 1825 but survived to be returned to Sydney with seven other sick prisoners in May of 1827. Green then lived in Liverpool for decades, dying in 1872, aged seventy-three years.

Location was another difficulty the settlement faced. Whilst Point Barlow was an easily defensible site for standard European-style naval attacks,[49] it was too far down Apsley Strait, the entry of which is fraught with dangerous shoals, to be of much use for anything. It was also so far from the normal sea lanes that few ships' captains were ever likely to venture there. Blainey[21] described the Fort Dundas settlers 'as marooned as a bug in a bottle.' As it turned out, Bremer's choice of site for the settlement was a poor one indeed.

124

In 1827, the new settlement in Raffles Bay was an attempt to be closer to where the Macassans visited annually to collect trepang whilst at the same time, maintain a military garrison in the region. Even so, when thirty-four prahus visited Raffles Bay during the 1828–29 season, the English had nothing to trade with them. Also, the Dutch so monopolised the on-selling of trepang that the fishermen were not allowed to sell any of it to the English anyway. And, after all, Fort Wellington was just a military garrison inhabited by a small wretched band of ill soldiers and convicts—why would anyone want to go there?

In May 1829, Sir George Murray, Secretary of State for the Colonies, sent Governor Darling his final orders concerning the northern coast:

"… the Settlements have proved unhealthy, difficulty in supplying them with provisions, and much annoyance is experienced from the natives. These objections are very serious, and I do not think that there is, on the other side, any prospect of advantage sufficiently strong to warrant a continuance of the Expense and risk of life, by which the Settlements have been established at Melville Island and Raffles Bay, must be maintained. You will therefore, upon receipt of this dispatch, proceed to withdraw the Troops and Convicts who have been stationed there."[99]

When the British sailed away from Raffles Bay in late 1829, the north of Australia was left alone by their countrymen for nearly a dozen years. The British had found themselves inflexible and lacking the right skills, the environment inhospitable, the local Aborigines unwelcoming, and their diet of salted meat, flour, dried peas, and grog often led them from weakness to sickness and sometimes to death. As a result, life in the settlements was particularly hard. We can only imagine the feelings of relief the settlers had when at last they sailed away from their lonely outposts and returned to civilisation.

11

THE ARCHAEOLOGY

Fort Dundas was never 'lost.' The early settlers in the Northern Territory, when settlement was finally successful, knew the history of European attempts to set up a presence in the area. Fort Dundas was the first of four failed attempts, the first three of which were military garrisons. The second, Fort Wellington, lasted only two years and was opened whilst Fort Dundas was in decline, and closed just a few months after Fort Dundas. Eleven years after that, Victoria Settlement was established on the shores of Port Essington, and it lasted longer. However, again, the winning formula for settling the north was elusive, and Victoria Settlement was closed in 1849.

These northern outposts ended up being temporary, and as they never intended to promote colonisation of a northern territory, the documents relating to them are not considered founding proclamations for the current Northern Territory. Colonization, in this respect, did not happen until civilians started to become more involved. In 1864, Lieutenant Colonel Boyle Finniss led a group of volunteers and land investors to settle at Escape Cliffs, near the mouth of the Adelaide River, in the fourth attempt at settlement. This attempt also failed, and the settlers endured three years of bitter in-fighting and poor management before withdrawing.

Finally, on 5 February 1869, George Goyder, the Surveyor-General of South Australia, brought a hundred and thirty-five people to Port Darwin and established a small settlement, which he named Palmerston, on the shores of a bay which had already been named *Port Darwin* by Captain Wickham of the Beagle, after his old shipmate, Charles Darwin. The naturalist never actually came close to this part of the world, but his name is now synonymous with north Australia as, at last, the settlement, now known as *Darwin*, prospered and still does today, as the capital of the Northern Territory. From the new settlement, the settlers soon had time to explore and exploit the resources they found all around them, and wonder about the earlier attempts at settlements.

Melville Island is just a few hours journey by boat north of Darwin, and by the turn of the twentieth century was a relatively easy place to travel to.

Some came to harvest the descendants of the Asian water buffalos, which had escaped from the settlement and run wild. The most famous of them all were Joe and Harry Cooper who arrived in 1895. At that time, any Tiwi who were alive during the time of Fort Dundas would have been very aged indeed.

Pearlers came to the islands as well. Along the southern coast, there was a pearling industry boom during the 1880s and again in 1895.[45]

Others came as tourists. The author Alfred Searcy was one of the early tourists to make it to Fort Dundas. In 1895, he was part of a party large enough to require four luggers. Together they sailed up through the straits and moored in King Cove to explore the ruins:

"Landing on some very slippery rocks, we made our way through

the mangroves up a short rise, and then saw what we at first took for a watercourse. Upon following it round, however, it dawned upon us that it was a real moat, with earth-works and bastions above it. So this was Fort Dundas, constructed some 70 years ago, I suppose to resist the attacks of the native...

Following a walled roadway out of the pit, we walked inland through parklike country, some of the trees being very fine. About half a mile away we came upon the ruins of what had evidently been a very substantial building. We put it down as the church*, as there were several places near it marked out with stones which looked like graves."[121]

Searcy doesn't record if he or his party collected any souvenirs from the Fort.

Then, in 1906, the first Catholic Mission was set up on the south west of Bathurst Island, at Nguiu, and the Tiwi, who up until then had little contact with the outside world, found their lifestyle rapidly changing.

In 1937, the government built a settlement right on the site of the Fort Dundas gardens. They maintained the name, Garden Point, but its function was to supply rations such as tea, sugar, and flour to local Tiwi, rather than grow food. The settlement grew to become a Catholic Mission and a home for mixed-race children, who later became known as part of the 'stolen generation,' from all over the Northern Territory. The Garden Point barge landing, built in the 1940s, is supposed to have been constructed partly by using bricks and rocks from the Fort Dundas settlement, especially those that made up the old wharf.

A medical team conducting a health survey of Melville Island spent time fossicking for artefacts at Fort Dundas in 1938. Some of their finds, such as buckles, buttons, and chin-strap buttons found their way to the State Library of New South Wales in 1972. A few

---

*   There is no mention of a church in any of the early writings. The 'substantial' building with a few graves nearby may also have been a hospital (Crosby 1975) or a military building supporting a watchtower (Woolfe 2001).

other finds have ended up, rightly, in the Northern Territory Museum collection, and one, a single musket ball, was one of a collection of relics of the North's past incorporated into the foundations of Darwin's War Memorial Cathedral, which opened in 1962.[56]

The first archaeologist to examine Fort Dundas in any detail was Eleanor Crosby[46] in 1975. Crosby and her team partly cleared much of the site and mapped all the features they could find (see Map 4) and then dug a trench through the eastern wall of the fort to look at its method of construction. She returned in 1978 to dig further trenches, examining one of the huts built by the convicts or marines. Her map is still useful—numbered metal tags she installed attached to star pickets can still orientate the visitor.

The next to come was Frederickson in 1999. He explored the commissariat store site, the possible location of the commandant's house, and the ruins, which everyone then assumed to be the hospital, but Searcy had called a church. Around the buildings his team found 2269 nails, 2174 pieces of broken glass, 378 pieces of ceramics, 168 bricks, and 69 clay pipe fragments. Wooden structures would naturally rot away and leave the nails behind, whilst the fragments of glass, pottery, and clay pipes would just lie on the ground as the detritus of everyday life and soon become buried and forgotten. More interesting items, such as a spoon and some metal buttons, a few musket balls and gunflints, a powder flask, a key, and a metal chisel were also brought to light.

Richard Woolfe[144] studied the site in 2001. He used GPS and other technology to examine the fortifications in terms of how well they could repel attackers.

Then came Colin De La Rue, who led three seasons of digs at the site from 2001, as part of his research program for Charles Darwin University.

Excavations are time consuming and expensive, and as a result, few and far between. The findings of these studies are, therefore, all the more valuable for their rarity, but still it was such a minor exploration of the site that we cannot yet assume to know as

130

much about the settlement as we could. Of course, after nearly two hundred years of the cycle of seasons, the settlement is now almost completely resumed by the forest. Huge trees have come and gone in that time, many of the elderly blowing down in cyclonic winds that rip them, roots and all, from the ground, their fallen logs later burning in dry season conflagrations. As a result, much of the top soil has been wrenched up and out, tilled by the roots, and then baked by the annual fires.

There is little to see at the site now: two or three low walls; the ditch that surrounded the fort and earth mounds behind it; the round turrets where the 9-pounder guns were mounted; a collapsed well; holes in the ground which were a sawpit and the magazine; a few unnaturally straight lines of rocks; a flat area near the sea which was the commissariat store site; scattered piles of rocks in the sea that appear at low tide which are the last remnants of the jetty; and one or two low grave mounds, are about all a casual visitor will find.

But archaeologists look harder. During Crosby's study, a number of slate stones were found near where the commissariat store was situated, and she concluded they were used on the roof. They must have been imported because there are no slate quarries anywhere on Melville Island. The slate is not mentioned in any of the known writings about the fort, so either the records have been lost, or the transport and use of such materials was so mundane as to not warrant a mention. The store was originally thatched, but there was a cyclone in 1827, which probably removed many of the rooves of the settlement. It is likely that the slate was installed on the store's roof to replace the thatch. Later, when the fort was abandoned, most of it may have been taken elsewhere because there are far too few pieces left on Melville Island for a whole roof[49].

Frederickson's team uncovered a large deposit of broken glass, pottery, and coal where the inside back wall of the commissariat store used to be. We can easily imagine the issuer, Mr Radford, or one of the convict servants, sweeping up anything broken, or dropped, on the floor and moving it out of the way.

Each of the teams of archaeologists added useful information to give us greater insights into life at the fort, but the starting point for all studies into the fort's history, naturally, are the few written sources from people who were there. Unfortunately, these journals, reports, and letters were written by members of a single strata of a highly stratified community—the commandants and others in command. Details about the soldiers and convicts, the minutiae of daily life, the designs of the huts, store room and hospital, what the woman and children did day by day, and much else of what makes a community were not recorded, so we have little to go on. This is compounded by the loss of two of Campbell's reports to the Colonial Secretary (numbers three and four) leaving a gap in the official record from December 1826 until April 1827. However, the authors give glimpses, albeit narrow and confined, into how parts of the settlement must have looked and operated at the time. Bremer was first:

> *"1st of October, a point being fixed to form the establishment, parties were sent on shore to clear the ground, and to lay the foundation of a fort... From the 1st to the 7th, parties employed clearing the ground, boats surveying, and the foundation of the fort going forward; the weather remarkable fine; Thermometer from 40˚ to 88. On the 8th began a pier for the purpose of landing the provisions, heavy stores, guns, &c. A Commissariat storehouse was commenced; and the officers' houses, which were brought from Sydney in frame, were began to be setup. From this period up to the 20th, the various works were carried on with such zeal, and perseverance, that the pier, one bastion, and the sea face of the fort was completed; and I had the satisfaction, on the 21st of October, of hoisting His Majesty's*

---

* This temperature range is as extraordinary as it is unlikely for October. In centigrade, it equates to 4°C-28°C! Whilst the latter is possible, Melville Island has probably never experienced temperatures as low as 4°C at any time of year.

132

colours, under a royal salute, from two 9-pounder guns, and one 12-pounder carronade, mounted on 'Fort Dundas' which I named in honour of the noble Lord, and the Head of the Admiralty. The pier is composed of immense heavy logs of timber, and large masses of sand stone rock; it is sixty-four feet long, eighteen feet wide, and thirteen feet high, at the end next low water-mark, and from the solidity of the materials, will probably last many years." [24]

The 'immense heavy logs' used in the construction of the pier and the fort were those cut down during the clearing of the site. Eucalypt trees dominated the forest when the settlers arrived, as they do today (mostly *Eucalyptus miniata* and *E. tetradonta*). Their trunks can be fifty centimetres or more in diameter, and despite being sometimes cored by the ubiquitous termites, their dense timber is hard and heavy. Bremer claimed that the daily temperature did not exceed about 28°C (88°F)[†], but convict gangs labouring to fell and split the timber, in the high humidity of the 'build-up' months of October and November, would have found the heavy work onerous. As time went on, and their poor diets started taking a toll, the work became even more difficult and the pace of building slowed markedly after the first industrious weeks, when it so impressed Bremer:

"The early annals of New South Wales will not, it is imagined, shew greater proportionate quantity of labour performed than that stated to be the result of the first day's operations— the clearing away of 450 trees. Already the construction of a respectable fort proclaims security from the attack of any ordinary foe. This fortification, situated upon Point Barlow, completely commands the harbour, the

---

[†]   The average temperature for Pirlangimpi in the month of October is 33.6°C and November 33.5°C, with maximum temperatures exceeding 38°C. This throws into doubt the temperature records made by Bremer. October is the hottest month of the year on Melville Island.

long guns (nine pounders) reaching Bathurst Island. Its dimensions are considerable. A ditch was digging 15 feet broad, and 10 deep. The works are formed of trees laid length ways, about 5 feet high, 7 feet broad at the base, and 5 feet at the top; the whole to be turfed over. Two very respectable habitations for the officers have already been erected within the fort, in which also the barracks are to stand. Immediately in front is the wharf, and to the left is a store-house.

King Cove, Port Cockburn, lies in long. 130. 27. 30. E. lat. 11. 25. S. Port Essington in long. 132. 10. E and lat. 11. 07. S. The channel of King Cove is represented as narrowed by sand banks, and it was feared that it could not be frequented at all seasons. A considerable portion of the land has been cleared, and a Battery erected. When the accounts left, twenty acres of timber were fallen, and the fort completed, with the exception of the ditch; it measures 100 yards by 80, the guns are mounted, consisting of two long nine pounders and four 18 pound carronades.

The magazine is also finished; Commissariat stores built, and provisions stored in it. Soldiers and prisoners hutted; a well sunk, and excellent water found at the depth of 30 feet." [24]

The 'two very respectable habitations for the officers,' which Campbell found to be 'extremely small and uncomfortable, being only temporary and hasty erections,'[33] were prefabricated houses shipped in frame from Sydney and put together inside the fort's walls. They appear in Smith's watercolour of the fort as small white rectangular huts, and a corner of one can be seen in Roe's 1824 sketch.

The fort was not designed to be a castle or a fortified town. It was a fort in the classical definition, where 'fort' meant a 'small fortification, made in a pass, near a river, or at some distance from a fortified town; to guard the pass, or to prevent the approach of ships, or an enemy by land.'[96]

Inside the fort's walls was a space some seventy meters by fifty meters in size, containing a sunken magazine, the officers' quarters, and two smaller structures of unknown function. The accommodation for the soldiers, marines and convicts, the commissariat store, the hospital, and all other structures, including the well, were outside. There was no emergency shelter for the populace inside the walls in case of a siege, and the barracks that Bremer mentioned may not have been constructed—none of the archaeologists found evidence for them. There were military barracks somewhere, as Campbell mentioned them as a place for refuge for the tattletale convict John Probyn, but we also know the soldiers and marines were required to build their own huts. They did this quickly in a row behind the fort, as the convicts worked on the government buildings and the well. The huts were 'good and comfortable cottages near the fort,' *The Australian* reported and:

> *"Oct. 17. The soldiers having completed their huts, most of them leave the ship to-day. The well which the prisoners have been digging, was discovered to have a large quantity of water in this morning, and very excellent it is."* [10]

The ruins are today in poor condition and few traces of the wooden huts remain. Crosby marked them on her map in a row on the eastern, inland, side of the fort. The ditch of the fort, which was so laboriously hacked out of the stony ground, has filled in to a greater or lesser extent, and the timbers used to shore up the sides and the huge horizontal logs are long gone, either burned or rotted away, leaving nought but a few traces of charcoal and some rusty iron nails.

De La Rue's archaeological excavations of the Fort Dundas site included three major digs over three seasons: the west 'curtain' wall; the southwestern turret; and a hollow within the fort's walls, which turned out to be a brick-walled, sunken magazine, complete with a few scattered lead musket balls. His choices of dig sites reflect his major focus of looking for evidence that the reasons for the existence of Fort Dundas leaned more towards its military purpose than trade/economic reasons.

De La Rue's analysis shows how the fort's close proximity to the beach, raised a little on the headland, gave it uninterrupted fields of fire towards any ships journeying down Apsley Strait, and as he observed, the guns commanded the whole anchorage of King Cove. The nine-pounder guns would have easily reached Bathurst Island across the strait, and in fact, local folklore tells of people finding shot embedded in the cliffs of that island, across from Point Barlow. Standing on the point nowadays, peering through gaps in the mangroves and thick regrowth foliage, it is hard to imagine the clarity of the view as it must have been after the early clearing of the site done by the convicts in 1824. Roe's sketches of the time give us simple views of the settlement, just weeks after the first sod was turned, and we know what it looked like later through Campbell's 1827 map (see Map 3), measurements of ruins and artefact positions on the ground, and educated guesswork. The accuracy of Campbell's map is questionable, both in terms of scale and position of the buildings, but it gives us an idea of the sprawling nature of the settlement, which is confirmed by the distribution of artefacts and remnants of walls hundreds of meters from the fort. The fort drawn on the map would have been huge, much larger than the ditches it left behind. Also, several mystery buildings are marked, but searches to find them by the archaeologists have been unsuccessful. For example, Crosby looked for a building marked south of the store, on the North West corner of the fort, without success.

There is further evidence of a low intent to develop the economic side of the settlement in the lack of any planning for bulk movement and storage of goods. It took two years before the original wharf was upgraded to be useable at all tides, and Campbell mentions the need for the construction of a 'government warehouse, in order that the first traders who venture here may find a place of safety in which to deposit their goods.'[35] This warehouse was probably never built. In 1826, Campbell was newly arrived, of course, so may have still been looking at the settlement through rose-coloured glasses.

136

No traders had yet visited, and it took him a few months to realise that it was unlikely that any traders would ever appear in the strait. Captain William Barns was there, of course, probably the man keenest on the commercial side of the settlement since before its instigation, but after the loss of the *Stedcombe* he was a spent force, and seems to have become little more than a thorn in the side of the commandants. Barns was a civilian unconnected to any of the military. He was, perhaps, one of the only true 'settlers,' albeit in the end, a reluctant one in a settlement which really remained just a military outpost.

Woolfe[144] reports on fieldwork by Dr Clayton Fredericksen, Colin De La Rue, and David Steinberg in 2001. Using 'predictive modelling techniques,' they measured line-of-sight fields of view, both from the fort and from rumoured gun locations on the north coast of the tiny Harris Island in the middle of the straits. From this research, Woolfe also suspected that there might have been an extra lookout built upon either Luxmore Head or a site a kilometre south of the fort that gave an uninterrupted view up the strait.

After his examination of the 'west curtain' wall and ditch, De La Rue concluded that the fortifications were well designed to resist European style artillery bombardment but not attacks by infantry. It seems the settlers' fears were more directed towards other European navies than foot soldiers, and if they'd been attacked overland by a sizeable-armed Malay force, or even organised Tiwi raiders, the walls would have hardly slowed them down. The fort's walls and the turrets were timber structures filled with soil and rocks excavated from the ditches in front of them. They were sturdy earthworks with ramparts that were cored and reinforced by timber, but agile attackers would have quickly been able to scale them. Nevertheless, the bulk of earth rock and stone held within the ramparts would have coped well with cannon fire, particularly from the awkward angle of a ship mounted weapon. The walls were also covered in narrow 'glacis' that providing an upward sloping area in front of the rampart whose purpose was to bounce any low flying shot over the fort, rather than allowing it to plough into the rampart[49].

Both Woolfe and De La Rue concluded that the fort's primary purpose was for European style military defence and, when considering the few agricultural and industrial possibilities of Melville Island at the time, believe that there never was any other real purpose. Bremer's stated reasons for the fort's design thus held little reality:

> "... and as it was probable the Malays would visit the place in great numbers, and as much hostility might be expected from the natives, who were as we could judge, from the number of their fires on both islands to be very numerous, I was determined to render the fort as strong as the means of the expedition would admit."[25]

The usual fort design from the period in areas where the enemy was expected to be lightly armed without artillery was a wooden stockade or palisade[126], and indeed, this is what Captain Smyth built at Fort Wellington, in Raffles Bay, only a few years later[123]. Bremer clearly designed the fort to face a European foe and not the potential enemy he identified on paper.

De La Rue's excavation of the south-turret was undertaken to evaluate how ready the fort was for using its guns. The long-range nine-pounder cannons were deployed in the turrets but it appears they were standing on earth floors alone. The archaeologist had expected to find evidence of a wooden floor, or a mounting, because handling the cannons on dry dirt would be difficult, but they would have been nearly impossible to manoeuvre in wet season mud. However, there were no iron or copper nails buried in the ground indicating that there was never a hard decking there. Perhaps the turrets were never finished as no threats ever appeared from the sea.

De La Rue found that the magazine was of sufficient size to hold the quantity of powder and ammunition left behind by Bremer— 'fifty rounds of round shot, and Eight of Grape and Case' for each gun. The latter were for five, twenty-pounder carronades, which were mounted along the walls of the fort as a defence against small boats and bodies of men. This was a relatively paltry amount of ammunition. De La Rue says it cannot have sustained a long battle and compared it to a British nine-pounder field gun that carried a hundred and sixteen rounds into battle on a gun carriage and limber. Any battle at Point Barlow would have been unlikely to have lasted more than half a day. Of course, an invading force would not have known how little ammunition the marines and soldiers actually had, or that the carronades actually did not fit the long-gun carriages that had been supplied for them in error so were useless.

Bremer had also left a smaller 'boat gun' at the fort. This was a more portable metre-long carronade that could be mounted on the settlement's supply ship when it was travelling, as indeed it was: Spillett found this gun at Kampung Tutuwawang on Babar Island, still in the possession of descendants of the pirates who had pillaged it in 1824.

There was a random scattering of lead musket balls spread through the rubble of the magazine. De La Rue surmises that the roof of the magazine collapsed whilst it was still being used and that someone had had to partially excavate it to get the equipment out. The musket balls appear to have been dug out and swept up with the rubble and left behind. This seems reasonable because any roof that relied for its strength on timber would not have lasted long once termites discovered it. Water was another problem the settlers would have had with the magazine. The archaeologists found that the original entrance was modified and concluded that, once the rains started in November or December of 1824, the original ramped entrance way would have acted as a funnel, collecting water and directing it straight into the sunken room. Keeping powder dry must have been an ongoing problem for the marines.

De La Rue also speculates that the magazine may have been the 'dry well' within which Tambu Tipungwuti had been held after his capture in 1827 and, if it had started to collapse and become unusable by that time as a magazine, this is certainly possible.

Examining foundations and rocks still lying in rows gives little idea of what the building above them would have looked like. The commissariat store apparently didn't even have post holes as no remnants or marks were left behind. It may always have been built as a temporary construction; despite the fact it was probably given a slate roof after its original thatch was blown away. We know the store had a loft and double windows that needed to be locked, as they were mentioned during the convict Simpson's trial for stealing gin, and we know how big it was (eighteen meters by five meters) but little else for sure. The store appears on Roe's 1824 sketch (see figure 2) with its roof labelled 'thatch' and twice more in other views from across King Cove: the first appeared as a book illustration by Roe in 1827[75], and the second in a water colour by Smith (see Figures 3 and 4). Both these artworks show a rectangular building just above the high water mark with a door opening to a small dock crane and two small side windows, but otherwise they could be of different buildings—one looks small with an arched doorway like a church, the other looks larger, with a rectangular doorway. And neither looks like a building that was eighteen meters long. The two artworks are so similar in many other ways, even down to the angle of the flag and the position of the *Lady Nelson* in the cove that one may have been taken from the other. In the sketch by Captain Bunn, who also gives us a plan of the fort, the commissariat storehouse hardly appears at all (see Figure 1).

Thirty five years after Fort Dundas, the settlers at Escape Cliffs also built a store and one of the earliest known photographs from the Northern Territory shows it as a high-roofed log cabin, which was thatched with grass. The Fort Dundas commissariat may have looked much like this but with loft window shutters on the upper wall.

The numerous huts that housed the population, the hospital and other buildings are similarly hard to describe for lack of evidence.

140

We are not even sure if the building Crosby called the 'hospital' was a hospital at all. Dr Turner said the hospital was a weatherboard building large enough to contain sixteen beds.[138] He didn't mention

Figure 12 The store at Escape Cliffs, 1864. The wooden structure with its grass roof may give an idea of what the Fort Dundas commissariat looked like 40 years earlier. This is one of the earliest photographs from the Northern Territory, (courtesy State Library South Australia).

stone walls, so there may be nothing left of the hospital now but nails buried in the ground beneath where it stood.

Some have called the stone building remnants towards the east of the site a church. But Woolfe suggests it may have had a military purpose, because, if it was four or five meters tall, it would have had an uninterrupted view of Luxmore Head where a lookout could have been placed for a view north, up the straits[*].

Most buildings were probably simple bough structures, almost certainly with rooves of thatched grass, as 'grass cutting' is mentioned several times in the journals, but there were huts at Escape Cliffs, in 1864, which were roofed with wooden shingles, and this may have been the case on Melville Island also. Possibilities for the construction of the walls which weren't made of rocks include wattle and daub,

---

[*]   There is a painting by Owen Stanley from 1848 of a wooden observation tower, about 4 meters high, at Victoria Settlement.

Figure 13 Ruins of the stone building with dimensions of about 8mX6m. Many of the original rocks were removed by the builders of the original Garden point barge landing in the early 1940s.

shingles, hessian, or sheets of *Eucalyptus* bark. The Tiwi used sheets of bark for shelters and the British would have seen them.

When Campbell arrived, he said many structures were constructed of 'unsubstantial materials,' and he ordered more than several to be torn down and rebuilt. This is not surprising, as bush shelters would have been eaten out by termites and severely weathered by the tropical climate, in the two years since they had been hastily built. Straight lines of rocks may identify several building sites as foundations, or the edges of earth platforms upon which some of the huts might have sat above the wet season mud. But without postholes or other remnants it is impossible to determine what was there. We can locate the rough position of the blacksmith's shed down near the water's edge, as the roof is visible and labelled, in Roe's sketch.

More will be learned with each succeeding archaeological study of the site if the finance and the will are there to undertake them. The trouble is there may be not much of interest left. The artefacts are numerous, but have little variety—mostly nails and broken

142

pottery, so there is limited appeal in digging them up. The settlement was abandoned over several months, and equipment was slowly transferred to Fort Wellington. When the *Amity* loaded the last of the settlement's inhabitants and their belongings in February 1829, they would have made sure that nothing of value was left behind.

During the weeks following the British sailing away, curious Tiwi probably wandered through, picking at the detritus of the first European settlement in North Australia. What would their thoughts have been? Victory? Relief? We will never know as nothing was recorded, and it was another seventy years before more Europeans came back to the islands.

In the 1930s, more than a hundred years after the convicts' gardens were abandoned, the land on Garden Point was occupied by the government as a supply centre. Then, in 1941, a Catholic Mission was established to take charge of all Catholic Aboriginal children from The Bungalow, Alice Springs, and Kahlin Compound in Darwin. A residential school operated at the mission for children aged five to seventeen years. In later years, these children were to become known as part of what was called the 'stolen generation.'

Father Frank Flynn visited the mission from Darwin in the early 1960s and wrote of seeing the old brick kiln near where the gardens were. He said that many of the bricks were still in excellent condition and they were used in the baker's oven in the mission kitchens. Later, an Italian builder named Manlio Petrochi incorporated some more bricks and rocks from the fort into a statue and fountain at the school. There is no sign of the kiln in the community today, or indeed, of the statue and fountain, and the bakery was burned down a few years ago.

Father Flynn also reported finding a rum bottle with the government engraving of King George IV and 'a few old coins' on an earlier visit, but said there was nothing like that there when he returned in 1962[56].

The community was called 'Garden Point,' and it still is on airline maps. It became known as 'Pularumpi' in the 1970s, but since the

1990s it has been called 'Pirlangimpi.' Only the school still bears the name 'Pularumpi' because the Principal at the time resisted any name change and found support from the community to retain the old name:

"Why change the school's name? Can't it be *Pularumpi School, Pirlangimpi*?" I said.

12

FORT DUNDAS 2016

By March 2016, the wet season had disappointed most residents of the Top End. Everywhere the rain had been patchy – the flood plains of the great rivers had never really flooded and the weathermen were already calling it the driest wet on record. Melville Island, however, has *Hector,* Hector is a reliable and productive cloud mass, which forms above the centre of the island and moves westward nearly every day in the season, wringing from its grey skirts huge amounts of water. Unlike everywhere else across the Northern Territory, the rainfall stats from Pirlangimpi Airport weren't falling short.

Hector's best efforts fell in full fury the day I managed to return to the forested site of Fort Dundas. Rain made the forest seem to press in closer, as if the trees were huddling together like lovers under a single umbrella. But it wasn't cold and we weren't going to let the rain interfere in our exploration. As we arrived, the rain was easing anyway. I was with Brett, a resident of Pirlangimpi with an interest in its history. He had visited the fort before but had seen little more than the ditch and was keen to explore it in more detail; although he did wisely suggest that we should return in the dry season, after the scrub had been burned off. Nevertheless, he had been happy to give me a lift to the fort in his battered Toyota and had driven through the heavy rain cheerfully.

I wrapped my camera in a plastic bag and climbed down from the truck. We had stopped right at the end of the track, just meters from the final rocky remnants of the Fort Dundas jetty. It was nearly high tide, and there wasn't anything that would tell anyone who wasn't looking for it that there was something of historical interest there at all. Across the Apsley Strait, the water was calm, but blurred as the rain drops splashed gaily across the surface.

When I lived in Pirlangimpi and worked as the head teacher of Pularumpi School twenty years before, the vehicle track to the site had ended several hundred meters inland in a small parking area, formed by a fence of treated pine logs. A small preservation grant had allowed someone to construct it in an attempt to protect the site a few years earlier. They had also spent time cutting down and removing some of the trees that had been growing through the remaining walls, and they had fenced the well with high metal posts and wire to stop animals and people falling in.

But someone too lazy to walk had driven through the pine log fence, and his one track had become the access road, right through the site. I hadn't noticed the old carpark, as we drove through, as it was hidden by the rain and the thick wet season growth, so I was surprised to see the sea when we reached it.

At first, I was not really sure where we were. The new road had thrown me. Twenty years ago, I could have walked the site blindfolded. I had run an English language program with my Pularumpi School students called "Tour Guides,".We had studied the fort's history in class and then learned the English required to show other people around the site, knowledgeably sprouting facts and stories of the fort. It was a wonderful opportunity for the kids to learn some local history, and they did indeed give guided tours to their parents and other classes from the school.

The rain eased, and taking my bearings from the jetty from memory and wishing I'd remembered to bring along a copy of Eleanor Crosby's 1975 archaeological sketch map,[46] I took some guesses.

"The fort is just over there," I said, pointing into the forest to the south of the track. "Which means the well is just a few meters over this way to our left. The storehouse was just down here on the flat, beside the sea."

The rain stopped as I pushed into the scrub towards the fort. Brett had been there before but hadn't yet found the well, so he decided to look for it first.

Some twenty or thirty meters into the forest I easily found the north western corner of the moat. Ditches ran straight in two directions at right angles to each other. Two hundred years ago at this corner sat a twenty pounder cannon. The archaeologists had found no evidence of any wooden or stone footings for it and now, after the rain, the ground was very soft. If the cannons had ever been used after rain, they would have been difficult to control on such a mushy surface without any footings.

Brett's search for the well had been unsuccessful so he joined me in the moat, and together we climbed the western ramparts. I was keen to find the sunken magazine—the collapsed brick roofed structure which had been along this side of the fort. Everywhere the wet season growth carpeted the ground but after a little searching Brett called out in triumph:

"Over here," he said. "Bricks."

Sure enough several bricks that had been carefully placed were still in position. De La Rue's excavation here had found that the magazine had indeed been sunken, and the distribution of musket balls and other detritus showed that at one time part of it had collapsed and been repaired with a new entrance way.[49] The archaeologists had filled in their excavations, of course, so now nothing was visible apart from these few bricks. The Fort Dundas brick makers were led by Henry Feathers, the free man, and included the convicts Thomas

Marrot and James Tree who had both been thieves. The bricks were probably placed in this position in 1824, by the convict bricklayers Alfred Abbot, a chicken thief, and Charles Green, who had been sentenced for breaking and entering. Looking at their work, I was pleased to recall that all these men had survived their time on Fort Dundas and a few had even lived well into old age.

I confidently offered to lead Brett to the well.

"Follow me," I said. "It's just over here."

Indeed it was, but we marched right passed it in the undergrowth, and it was a full half an hour searching before we found it. While exploring, we found some of Crosby's metal tags on short star pickets, now heavily rusted. Number 51 marked three or four rocks, which looked aligned—and therefore not natural. This was, she said, the edge of a platform for a hut within which dwelled a marine, perhaps, with his family. In a line, we also found numbers 52 and 53.

Brett had found a depression earlier, and he asked if that was the well.

"No," I replied. "The well is unmistakeably a well."

About three meters in diameter, it drops at least four meters with almost straight sides. Its original diameter was reported to be only 2 metres, and it had been almost 10 meters deep. Photos I took twenty years ago show there has been a partial collapse of one of the sides since, and several large boulders now sit on the bottom of the well. Gideon Pangiramini, the grade seven school captain in 1997, had climbed down the pit using strong tree trunks and roots which formed a kind of ladder, but these were now gone. He had found a wallaby skeleton down there. The collapse of large boulders suggest that descending into the well is fraught with danger, but I wondered what archaeologists would find if they dug to the bottom.

"It seems to me," I said to Brett, "that if people were abandoning the fort to the Tiwi, anything they didn't take with them would be thrown down the well".

"It'd be a difficult excavation," he agreed. "The sides would

148

Figure 14 The 1996 Pularumpi School Captain, Gideon Pangiramini, at the bottom of the dry Fort Dundas well.

have to be shored up well, or the diggers could be buried themselves."

The 1975 fence they built to avoid accidents or tragedies is nowadays in complete disarray. Only a single post stood in its correct position, and the wire it once supported curled uselessly around and among the grass. A sign that once hung on it was now more rust than sign.

I wanted to see Sophie Hicks's grave and had some vague recollection of where it was, so I suggested I walk back up the track to where the fenced parking area had once been, with Brett bringing up his truck behind me. It was pleasant walking indeed. With the rain over the birds had come out in force for their evening song and the sun came out, low in the west, lighting a million stars among the dripping leaves.

Some of the treated pine 'copper' logs of the fence were still there, though now blackened and mostly burned away. The people who had made the new track had lifted one side of one of them out of the ground and swivelled it around like a gate to make a gap big enough to drive through.

I turned right and entered the bush again, sure that Sophie's grave was just a few meters away. Brett arrived and together we zigzagged

149

through the bush. I had an old memory of what it looked like—a reddish mound in the scrub. Then I suddenly had a feeling that I was about to be enveloped in thick fog. A white wall of fog seemed to be approaching through the trees. I peered closer. It wasn't fog, but paint. As we got closer the blindingly white sides of three enormous

Figure 15 Point Barlow and Fort Dundas today. The site is surrounded by the Port Melville Development.

diesel tanks appeared, each as big as a three storey building.

The tanks can easily be seen from the air, from far down the straits, when you fly from Bathurst Island to Melville. In fact, they stand out more than the community of Pirlangimpi itself. When full, they will hold ten million litres of diesel fuel each, and they are there to supply the controversial Port Melville development and passing ships that would rather refuel there than Darwin. Forestry is big business, and Port Melville had been recently constructed to ship out the woodchips and timber from the forestry plantations around Pickertaramoor in the central part of the island. Unfortunately the port's construction had been pushed through by the Government without the necessary environmental studies. Thirty-eight endangered species are at more risk because of the looming arrival of huge container ships collecting diesel from the port, and at the time of writing, the Government has admitted to

150

having acted unlawfully. When I was there, little was happening because of the uproar from the wider community and a court battle with the Environment Centre of the Northern Territory. The owners had had to suspend operation until the enquiry into the whole business had been completed, and it looks like, in the future, the port may well be approved to operate as a timber exporting facility, but not as a supply facility for diesel and oil.

There was a small ship moored to the wharf, and another sat idle out in the straights. Two men were fishing from the wharf.

Brett and I jumped a ditch and walked around the giant tanks. The forest had been cleared and a huge pile of woodchips had been brought in already from the plantations inland. The pile was behind a fence, but from under it came a torrent of black water carrying tannin from the woodchips. This is quite normal for a forestry operation, but this foul smelling black water was running into the sea. I took a photograph of it, letting lose my inner eco-warrior.

We walked back the other side of the tanks and had almost jumped back over the ditch and re-entered the forest, but we were hailed:

"Hey, what are you blokes doing?"

One of the guys we had seen fishing had run up after us.

"Just having a look," I said.

"Did you go through the gate?" he asked. It was clear we hadn't. The port was a sensitive issue. Perhaps we *were* eco-warriors collecting evidence and hence were a threat.

"No, the forest. We're looking for a grave."

"I saw you taking photographs," he said. For a moment I considered jumping the ditch and disappearing into the forest, leaving him behind to describe the eco-warriors he hadn't been able to catch to his boss. But Brett was hoping to get work with the forestry company, so I thought better of the plan.

"Two hundred years ago an English woman named Sophie Hicks died just a few meters from here in childbirth. Her grave is here somewhere."

A second bloke arrived, driving a white ute.

151

"What's going on?" he asked.

"They say they're looking for a grave," said the first man.

"I know where the cemetery is, I'll take you."

"No, you don't understand. This grave is part of the Fort Dundas site, just here beside your fuel tanks." I told them a little of the story. It seemed that they had either never heard of the fort or had never bothered walking a hundred meters of so into the bush to see it. Maybe they weren't concerned that the development's huge clearing lays right beside the first European site in North Australia, and that its access road actually cuts through it.

I also made a suggestion:

"In 2024 it will be the bicentenary of the settlement. There'll be more interest in this site than ever before. You guys had better put up a fence to stop people like me wandering around the port."

Unsure what to do, they let us return to the forest. We hadn't yet found the grave but returned to the truck anyway and set off back along the track. But then, only 50 meters of so from where we parked, I saw the walls of the stone building we'd missed in the rain on the way in.

It was labelled as site number 62. The half meter thick walls showed a building which had been eight by six meters in size but now they were in a poor state—many of the rocks had been taken during the construction of the Garden Point barge landing, and the highest part of the remainder was only about a meter high. This is the building Searcy thought may have been a church, as there are graves just near it. Crosby called it an armoury because of the thick walls but it may also have been the base of an observation tower. Nobody really knows.

One of the graves belongs to Sophie Hicks. We had found it! Well, maybe, because there was no headstone or grave markings like the residents of Victoria Settlement famously left behind a few years later, but this is the grave everyone attributes to her. Other graves found in this area belong to the victims of scurvy or fever, or like Julius Campbell and Dr Gold, Tiwi spears. The Northern

Territory Genealogical Society had erected a brass marker beside Sophie's grave, which lists those who had died at the fort: "Rest in Peace" it says and:

> *"This plaque commemorates the last resting place of those who served and those who came to Fort Dundas (1824-1827). Transfer of this settlement to Fort Wellington occurred in the early part of 1828"*

Unfortunately, the authors misdated the departure by a year as the last settlers actually left in February 1829. They also incorrectly dated Lorien's death and left one of the dead marines, poor Richard Thomas, off the list entirely. But they meant well, and at last the settlers were receiving some recognition, albeit on a lonely plaque placed in the bush. In all, at least thirty-five European and African settlers had perished at the Fort, including Sophie Hicks's baby, and at least one Tiwi man was killed in a skirmish because of the settlement.

The Tiwi Land Council supported the commemoration and the plaque continues after the list of the dead:

> *The owners of these lands in one accord with the Northern Territory Government acknowledge and respect the research of the Genealogical Society of the Northern Territory to record this last resting place of thirty three pioneers who came to these islands in the 1820's to establish a trading post and to protect our shores and who remain among us through our common eternity. Nimpangi mamanta nuwa nguriyi. Proudly sponsored by Northern territory Government.*

The ceremony that accompanied the placement of the plaque involved some dancing and the erection of two carved *pukumani* mortuary poles, which were left there, flanking the plaque.

Brett and I spent a few minutes pulling little tree saplings and vines out of the gaps in the walls. Too little too late, but cut stumps

Figure 16 The Fort Dundas commemorative plaque is flanked by pukumani mortuary poles.

were signs others had done just that within the last year or two, so we thought if someone came along every year and did the same, what was left might survive a few more decades.

We were soaked and muddy, but not yet finished. I wanted to speak with one of the traditional owners of the area, a man I knew well when teaching at Pularumpi School, because he was also a teacher there. Brett knew where to find him. Pirlangimpi Club only opens a couple of times a week, and many of the community members would be there drinking the permitted mid-strength beer. Brett and I climbed in the truck and rattled our way back to town.

I recognised his deep velvety voice as soon as I arrived from within the crowd.

"*Gela*," he called me. "Welcome home…"

We shook hands warmly. Patrick Puruntatameri had taught me much in my first role of a bush school head-teacher in the 1990s. He was one of the first Aborigines to graduate as a teacher in the Northern Territory and was a natural educator —calm, knowledgeable, with an extraordinary command of English and his mother-tongue, Tiwi. He knew everything about the kids and their families, and

154

how the community operated.

Patrick is proud of how his ancestors met and rebutted the first English settlers two hundred years ago. Tall and slim, he had recently turned 65 years old, but was still as ramrod straight as a drill sergeant. As a respected elder in the Tiwi community, he knew everything that was going on. He led me around the beer garden. Everyone remembered me, but I needed help recognising some of the now adult faces I hadn't seen since they were young. I was filled in with the gossip—whom had married whom, where people were now, who had had babies. Of course, many people mentioned Cyril Rioli, a community champion now playing football for Hawthorn in Melbourne. I repeated a few stories of him as an eight year old in my grade 4 class. Laughing with them, I realised how much I had missed this community in the twenty years since I had left.

Patrick and I sat at his customary table and talked of old times. Then of Fort Dundas. He remembered the history we had researched with the kids twenty years before.

"There is a dance that men do here that tells of those times," I said.

"Yes, the sailing boat dance," he said immediately. "You have seen it."

He stood up and briefly went into the pose of the dance, holding his arms like the sails of tall ships. I had an image of Tiwi warriors dancing this way on the stomping ground at ceremonies in the nineteenth century. This dance, Patrick claimed, has been passed on unchanged since it was first performed by his ancestors in the 1820s. Young people around me agreed. They knew it, and would perform it at ceremonies for the rest of their lives, and so would their children. They had danced it at the ceremony beside Sophie's grave when the memorial plaque had been unveiled.

Everyone also knew about Tambu Tipungwuti, the Tiwi man who had been captured by the soldiers, chained, and held captive in a hole in the ground for a few days until his escape. The Tipungwuti clan is still strong on Melville Island. They are proud of their ancestor, particularly so because so few ancestors' names are known in Tiwi culture.

"What do you think of Port Melville being so close to *Punata*?" I asked, using the Tiwi name for Point Barlow.

"Ah, that's no good, no good," Patrick replied. "The fort is history for Tiwi people as well as Australia. It should be better protected, but no money, hey."

"The fort isn't heritage listed yet by the government. Why is that?"

"I don't know," he replied. I had heard that the Tiwi Land Council had resisted any attempt by the Norhern territory Heritage Council to have it listed, but no one I had spoken to about it knew why, and Patrick didn't know, either.

We chatted on about the future of the site. Could it become a tourist destination? There's not much there to see, but with some judicious land clearing and imagination it may prove to be an interesting site, and bring much needed employment and income to the community. There was a whole class full of tour guides trained to show people around the site in 1997. More could be done—perhaps with the looming bicentenary it will be, as interest grows.

The next afternoon, as the Air North plane took off over King Cove and Point Barlow, I looked down to see the tops of trees in a forest that looks as though it has never been disturbed. The British soldiers, marines, and convicts who had worked so hard to establish a new settlement with an initial burst of enthusiasm and industry had been worn down within weeks as a result of their poor diets, the climate, the isolation, and the unwelcoming Tiwi. Some had to wait nearly five years before they could leave, others are still there in scattered graves across the point. But viewing *Punata*/Point Barlow from the air that day, it was as though they had never been there at all.

APPENDICES

Appendix 1: List of Ship's Company

List published in *The Monthly Magazine or British Register Vol LX part 11 for 1825 p302:*

> "Names of the Officers attached to the Expedition to Melville and Bathurst Islands
>
> His Majesty's Ship Tamar*, Jas. John Gordon Bremer, Esq., K.C.B captain; John Golding, John Downey, John Septimus Roe, lieutenants: John Davis, second master; John O'Brian, purser; Matthew Capponi, surgeon; Henry Clayton and Charles Cartwright Williamson, lieutenants marine; Henry Ennis, (supernumerary purser); Joseph Chartres, assistant surgeon; James Strachan, gunner; James Stocker, boatswain; John Charters, carpenter; John Coney Sicklemore, Francis Smyth, Alfred Nelson Fairman, and Francis Scott, midshipmen; James

---

*   This list is not exhaustive: there was also an officer named Mills mentioned in journals and the crew is not named.

Kirkpatrick, Alfred Paul, and Robert Campbell Jackson, volunteers; Frederick Henry Glasse, master's mate; Samual Hood Linzee and John Fulford, admiralty midshipmen; William Gough Tomlinson, admiralty clerk; John Wilson, (acting) second master; Maurice Barlow, captain 3rd Regiment; -- Everard, ensign; ditto – staff: Mr _____*, surgeon; George Miller, commissary; Mr Wilson, commissary's clerk; Mr Talmash, store keeper.

Countess of Harcourt: George Bunn, captain; George Clayton, first officer; John McDonald, second officer; __ Hall, third Officer.

Lady Nelson: Samuel Johns, master."

APPENDIX 2: LIST OF OFFICERS AND MEN WHO WERE STATIONED AT FORT DUNDAS

THE 3ᴿᴰ REGIMENT OF FOOT

Captain Maurice Barlow, Commandant
Lieutenant Everard, Second in Command
Sergeant Henry Stewart
Private Samuel Hodder
Private Thomas Burley
Private John Flinn
Private George Farrell
Private James Polvine
Ensign Richard Nugent Edwards
Private Patrick Burke
Private Benjamin Palmer
Corporals Murry and Carter were both listed in the Return of the Sick, Nov 1824 – April 1825, but it is not known if they were soldiers or marines.
Plus up to sixteen other men†

THE MARINES

Lieutenant Charles Cartwright Williamson
Sergeant John Brookshaw (died of cholera 31 Dec 1826)
Corporal Samuel Gwillan (died by spears 11 June 1825)
Private Reece Jenkins
Private Courtnay
Private William Bennett (died 6 June 1825, unspecified cause)
Private William Burton (died 10 November 1826, unspecified cause)
Private Richard Thomas (died 29 August 1825, unspecified cause)
Plus fifteen or more other men and three wives and four children.

---

† Privates Edward Oakly and Joseph Churchill drowned in a small boat accident at Port Essington.

THE 57ᵀᴴ REGIMENT OF FOOT

Major John Campbell
Captain Humphrey Robert Hartley
Lieutenant John Ovens
Lieutenant William Bate
Sergeant Newbolt
Corporal Thomas Allen
(Acting) Corporal Thomas Foley
Private Daniel Leonard
Private George Rowe
Private William Dyer
Private William Sadleir
Private Richard Calvert
Private Edward Pembrick
Private Warren
Private John Bailey
Private Patrick Brown
Private Richard Dooley (age 31)
Plus 24 other rank and file (including 2 drummers)
Plus several wives and children.

HMS LADY NELSON

Captain Samuel Johns
Plus nine crewmen, (all killed by islanders in February 1825).

HMS MERMAID

Captain Samuel Nolbrow
And about twelve crew.

APPENDIX 3: LIST OF CONVICTS WHO SERVED AT FORT DUNDAS

Family Name	Given Name	Age at court	Crime	Sentence	Occupation	Time on Melville Island	Fate
Abbott	Alfred	19	Stealing chickens	7	Bricklayer	May 1826	Sydney 1829, died 1857
Alexander	William	32	Homicide	14	Stone mason	1828? – Feb 1829	Sydney 1828, died 1857
Anglin	John	23	?	7	Shoe maker	May 1826	Served at Raffles Bay then returned to Sydney, August 1829. Granted freedom 1831– end of sentence.
Baker	Jane	33	Grand larceny	14	Servant	Jan 1828 – Feb 1829	Returned to Sydney, died December 1829
Baptiste	Nicholas	45	Desertion (court marshalled)	Life	bandsman	Sept 1824 – death	Died of scurvy, 5/5/1825 at Fort Dundas.
Barton	Charles	19	Stealing chickens	7	Salt miner	May 1826 – Feb 1829	Died in Camperdown 1834.
Blanchard	Joseph	18	Burglary	Life	Carpenter	Sept 1824 – Feb 1829	Pardoned in Parramatta 1836
Boon	James	25	Burglary	Life	Errand boy / carpenter	Nov 1825 – Feb 1829	Pardoned Parramatta 1837. Died 1853, Balmain.
Brennan	Steven	16	Stealing trousers	7	Stable boy	Late 1826 – Feb 1829	Granted freedom 1834 – end of sentence.
Brown	James	18	Stealing lead	7	Plasterer	May 1826 – Feb 1829	Granted freedom 1829 – end of sentence, married 1830.
Bullock	James	19	Stealing a trunk of clothing	7	Errand boy / Servant	Sept 1824 – 1828	Lived in Wilberforce. Still alive in 1856
Campbell	Julius (Joshua)	31	Stealing clothing	7	Ship's steward	Sept 1824 – death	Killed by Tiwi, 26 Oct 1826.
Carty	William	20	Assault	7	Carpenter	Sept 1824 – 1827	Granted freedom in 1827 – end of sentence.
Carthy	Jeremiah	27	?	7	Painter and glazier	Sept 1824 – August 1828	Granted freedom 1830– end of sentence.

Cock	Thomas	49	Forgery	Life	Farmer and Brewer	Sept 1824 – Feb 1829	Died in Liverpool in 1877, aged 71 years.
Connor	Daniel	20	Absent from home after sunset (under Insurrection Act, Cork)	Life	Stone mason, setter and cutter	Sept 1824 – August 1828	Invalided out in 1828, Died 1838 of dysentery in Bathurst.
Cox	Thomas	?	?	7	Metal worker / sailor	Nov 1825 – Aug 1827	Granted freedom – end of sentence, and left Melville Island 1827 for Timor but returned for work. Sailed to Sydney 1828.
Crane	Thomas	32	Stealing horses, a cart and wheat	Life	Carpenter	Sept 1824 – March 1828	Unknown
Daly	William		Stealing shoes	7	Blacksmith	May 1826 – June 1828	Granted freedom October 1828– end of sentence.
Davis	Thomas	25	Burglary	Life	Sawyer	Sept 1824 – death	Died of scurvy, 14/8/1825 at Fort Dundas.
Donohoe	Joseph	20	Stealing lead	7	Servant	Aug 1828 – 1829	Went to Raffles Bay as servant to John Radford (Dep. Ass. Commissary General). Died 1838 NSW.
Doyle	James	16	Picking pockets	7	Cowboy	?? – Feb 1829	Transferred to Raffles Bay 1829. Granted freedom 1832 – end of sentence.
Faulkener	?	?	?	?	Boat builder	?	Granted freedom 1827 – end of sentence, went to Kupang? Ref: Reid 1995.
Firby	John	27	Burglary	Life	Tinman and brazier	Sept 1824 – Feb 1829 (?)	Died Sydney 1828.
Gibson	James	19	Stealing tobacco	7	Baker	Nov 1825 – Feb 1829	Granted freedom Sydney 1830 – end of sentence.
Green	Charles	20	Stealing cotton, breaking and entering	7	Bricklayer	Sept 1824 – Dec 1826	Granted freedom Sydney Dec 1826, died 1872 aged 73 years.

Handy	George William	21	Stealing clothes	Life	Servant	Sept 1824 – Aug 1826	Invalided out in 1828. Drowned whilst swimming at South Head in 1830.
Hawkins	William	16	Assault	7	Cooper	Nov 1825 – Feb 1829	Granted freedom in 1828 – end of sentence. Married in 1846
Healy	Patrick	22	Stealing money	7	Servant and groom	Oct 1826 – Nov 1828	Granted freedom 1833.
Hennington	Charles	21	Breaking and entering	Life	Shoemaker	Nov 1825 – Feb 1829	Conditional pardon 1846
Henrys	William	21	Stealing leather.	7	Carpenter/ stock keeper	August 1826 – Feb 1829	Died Maitland 1838 aged 34.
Holt	Charles	20	Stealing 10 shawls	7	Painter and glazier	Nov 1825 – Feb 1829	Granted freedom 1831 – end of sentence.
Houghlahan / Houlahan	William	34	Stealing 4 sheets	7	Shoemaker	1826 – Feb 1829	Transferred to Raffles Bay until August 1829. Granted freedom – end of sentence 1833.
Johnson	Henry	24	Stealing 2 jackets	7	Servant	Sept 1824 – death	Died of scurvy, 2/12/1826 at Fort Dundas.
Johnson	James		Stealing shoes and stockings	7	Seaman	Sept 1824 – Sept 1828	Invalided to Sydney
Johnson	Robert	22	Stealing a horse	Life	Baker	May 1826 – Feb 1829	Transferred to Raffles Bay Feb 1829. Returned to Sydney August 1829.
Kelly	James	33	Burglary	Life	Sailor	Sept 1824 – Feb 1829	Transferred to Raffles Bay Feb 1829. Returned to Sydney August 1829. Died 1859.
Kitt	Robert Christopher	17	Stealing money	Life	Plasterer's apprentice	Sept 1824 – death	Died of scurvy 28 March 1825 at Fort Dundas. Also had cancer.
Seaman	William Labrook	?	?	?	Colonial service?	?	?
Lee	John	17	?	Life	Stonemason apprentice	Sept 1824 – Feb 1829	Recorded at Parramatta in June 1829. Died (?) 1883, aged 90.

163

Lewis	James	19	Stealing a handkerchief	Life	?	? – August 1828	Invalided out in 1828 by Assistant Surgeon Sherwin.
Lorien	Joseph	27	Stealing tools	7	Mariner / labourer	Sept 1824 – death?	Reported lost in the bush 2nd October 1824
Lowther	Edward	23	Robbing	14	Wet cooper / sawyer	Nov 1825 – Feb 1828	Granted freedom 1839 – end of sentence.
Marriot	William	23	Receiving stolen poultry	14	Waggoner	Nov 1825 – Feb 1829	In 1836 was recorded as being in Bathurst
Marrot	Thomas	23	Stealing apparel	7	Brick maker	Nov 1825 – Sept 1828	Granted freedom Sept 1838 – end of sentence and returned to Sydney.
Marsden	John	32	Highway robbery	Life	Horse dealer	?	Married in 1829 in Bathurst
Mason	John	?	Robbery	7	Stock herder	Nov 1825 – Feb 1829	Granted freedom Sept 1829 – end of sentence, in Sydney.
McCarthy	Jeremiah	?	?		Labourer	Nov 1825 (?) – Aug 1828	Invalided out in 1828 by Assistant Surgeon Sherwin.
McCarthy	Michael		Stealing a handkerchief	Life	Plasterer, but was Assistant Gardener for the fort.	Nov 1825 – Feb 1828	Transferred to Raffles Bay Feb 1829 as gardener. Returned to Sydney August 1829. Granted freedom March 1832. Died 1865 aged 59 years at Liverpool.
Montgomery	John	23		Life	Cooper	Sept 1824 – Aug 1828	Invalided out in 1828 by Assistant Surgeon Sherwin. Conditional pardon 1840.
Moore	Richard	?	?	Life	White smith	Sept 1824 – death	Died 6/11/1825 at Fort Dundas. Possibly of scurvy, although he was admitted for 'contusions' (bruising).
Moxham	James	26	Uttering forged notes	14	Gun and breech maker	August 1827 – Feb 1829	Died June 848 in Argyle NSW, aged 55 years.
Nixon	William	18	Highway robbery	Life	Cotton spinner / dyer / wheelwright	Sept 1824 –	Died probably 1862 Sydney, aged 58 years.

Notley	Thomas	18	Stealing 3 silver tea spoons.	Life	Sawyer	Nov 1825 – ?	Ticket-of-leave awarded 1826 in Manning NSW. It seems he spent very little time at Fort Dundas. Conditional pardon 1839.
Oakley	Henry	19	Stealing a watch, a seal and a key.	Life	Carpenter apprentice	Sept 1824 – Aug 1828	Invalided out in 1828 by Assistant Surgeon Sherwin. Conditional pardon 1850. Died 1853 in Bathurst NSW.
Parker	Richard	42	Breaking and entering, stealing a coffee pot.	14	Sawyer	Sept 1824 – Feb 1829	Died Berrima Stockade 1835.
Parry	John	21	?	7	Cabinet maker	Sept 1824 – Sept 1828	Granted freedom Sept 1828 – end of sentence and returned to Sydney.
Pell	Robert Sallow	33	Stealing	Life	Seaman / labourer	Sept 1824 – ?	?
Pepper	John	28	Horse stealing	Life	Mariner	June 1827 – Feb 1829	Died probably 1860, aged 78 years, in Camperdown, NSW.
Phillips	William	14	Stealing goods	Life	Tailor's apprentice	Dec 1826 – Feb 1829	Transferred to Raffles Bay Feb 1829. Returned to Sydney August 1829. Granted freedom June 1834. Died 1838 in Sydney.
Plomer	Francis	19	Stealing chickens	7	Carpenter	Nov 1825 – death.	Died 10 March 1827, Fort Dundas, aged 21.
Price	Thomas	?	?	7	?	Nov 1825 – Feb 1829	Granted freedom 1832. Recorded in 1841 census as living at Port Phillip
Price	William	40	Stealing 2 saws and some lead.	7	Blacksmith	Sept 1824 – Dec 1826	Granted freedom Dec 1826 – end of sentence, in Sydney. Lived probably in Richmond after 1841.
Probyn	John	20	Burglary	14	Carpenter	Sept 1824 – Sept 1828	Granted freedom June 1837 – end of sentence.

Reale	Patrick	14	?	Life	Labourer	Sept 1824 – Feb 1829	Conditional pardon 1836. Living in Kurrajong for the 1841 census.
Regan	Matthew	27	?	Life	Labourer	Probably 1828 – Feb 1829	
Richardson	John Matthew	20	Stealing 3 bottles of gin.	7 and Life	Gardener	Nov 1825 – Feb 1829	Granted freedom 1837 – end of sentence. Died Maitland 1863, aged 66 years.
Roberts	William	17	Stealing a watch and 2 seals	14	Turner apprentice	Nov 1825 – Feb 1829	Granted freedom 1834 – end of sentence.
Robinson	Thomas	20	A felony	7	Sawyer	Sept 1824 – death	Died 25 August 1825 of scurvy at Fort Dundas, aged 25 years.
Rollinson or Rawlinson	Ephraim Thomas	19	House breaking	7	Nailer	Sept 1824 – death	Died 23 May 1825 of scurvy at Fort Dundas, aged 22 years.
Rycroft	Mary Ann	38	Stealing 2 gowns and a shawl.	Life	Dressmaker / servant	Aug 1827 – Feb 1829	Died 1857, in Sydney aged 69 years.
Sellers	Matthew	20	Stealing a watch, 1 seal and a key.	Life	Seaman	Probably 1828 – Feb 1829.	Transferred to Raffles Bay Feb 1829. Returned to Sydney August 1829. Died Liverpool May 1836.
Simpson	John	?	?	7	?	Sept 1824 – Aug 1828	Married 1831.
Skeldon	James	29	?	Life	Collier and quarryman.	Nov 1825 – Feb 1829	Died 1839, aged about 44 years, in Newcastle.
Smith	John	16	Breaking and entering.	Life	Copper plate printer	Sept 1824 – Feb 1829.	Living in Parramatta during 1843.
Sowerby	John	16	Using a forged bank note.	Life	Cabinet maker	Nov 1825 – Jan 1828	Died 1876, aged about 70 years, in Liverpool.
Spowage	William	16	Stealing a handkerchief.	7	Boat Builder	Nov 1828 – May 1826.	Granted freedom Aug 1828 as sentence expired and returned to Fort Dundas in Nov 1828 as a free worker.
Sullivan	Thomas	31	?	7	Gardener	Sept 1824 – death	Died 18 Sept 1826 at Fort Dundas of scurvy.

166

Swan	Thomas	21	?	7	Tailor	May 1826 – Feb 1829	No information
Taylor	Henry	21	Larceny	Life	Sawyer	May 1826 – Feb 1829	Died 1849, aged 80 years, Parramatta.
Thompson	Charles	34	Stealing shoes.	7	Seaman and Cook	Sept 1824 – death	Died 12 May 1825 of scurvy at Fort Dundas.
Tiernan	Patrick	30	Stealing money	7	Shoemaker	Sept 1824 – death	Died 25 January 1825 of scurvy at Fort Dundas.
Tree	James	23	Assaulting and stealing.	Life	Brick maker and layer	Sept 1824 – Aug 1828	Invalided out in 1828 by Assistant Surgeon Sherwin for 'constant attacks of scurvy'. Recorded living in Sydney in March 1842.
Westwood	John	21	Theft of sugar and cheese.	Life	Gun maker / quarryman	Sept 1824 – Aug 1828	Invalided out in 1828 by Assistant Surgeon Sherwin for 'constant attacks of scurvy'. Conditional pardon 1835
Wilkins	James	35	Breaking and entering	Life	Groom	Sept 1824 – Feb 1829	Conditional pardon 1831.
Williams	Samuel	21	Petit Larceny	7	Horse shoer / labourer	Nov 1825 – July 1827	Granted freedom 1827 – end of sentence.
William	Thomas	36	?	7	Cook	?	?
Wilson	Walter		Robbery and arson	14	Stone mason / soldier	Sept 1824 – Feb 1829	Granted freedom 1832 – end of sentence. Married Ann Rowland 1832.

Source of information: Street 2012, Campbell 1834, Roe 1824 and others.

167

APPENDIX 4: LIST OF THOSE WHO DIED AT FORT DUNDAS

When he arrived at the end of 1826, Campbell wrote that 'during the period of two years before my arrival eight soldiers and four convicts had died; but two of these had been drowned and one died from spear wounds given by the natives.' He seems he was wrong. Seven convicts (possibly eight) are listed as having died of scurvy in those years, plus an African convict was speared. There were also nine deaths among the marines and soldiers, some of which were probably from scurvy. The two drownings mentioned by Campbell happened in the boating accident at Port Essington, before the fleet arrived at Melville Island.

The Genealogical Society of the Northern Territory lists thirty-three members of the Fort Dundas population buried in the Fort Dundas Cemetery. Their names are displayed on a memorial plaque at the Fort Dundas site, placed carefully beside the probable grave of Sophie Hicks (although they missed marine Richard Thomas and Sophie's unnamed baby girl who died at birth). The crews of

Figure 17 The commemorative plaque.

the *Lady Nelson* and the *Stedcombe*, and those that died before they ever landed on Melville Island are not remembered on the plaque. In total, this is at least twenty-three more people whose death was a part of the attempt to settle the island.

Following is a list of the names we know of those who died at Fort Dundas, the date on which he or she died and their cause of death.

CONVICTS

Lorian (or Franks), Joseph, 1/10/1824, an African marine/labourer from London. (Died 'lost in the bush' after eating cycad fruit).

Kitt, Robert Christopher, 28/3/1825, an African plasterer from London (scurvy).

Baptiste, Nicholas, 5/5/1825, a court marshalled soldier, (scurvy).

Thompson, Charles, 12/5/1825, an African-American seaman and cook, (scurvy).

Robinson / Rawlinson / Rollason, Ephraim (or Thomas), 23/5/1825, a nailer (scurvy, aged 22 years.

Davis, Thomas, 14/8/1825, a sawyer (scurvy, aged 25 years).

Moore, Richmond (or Richard), 6/11/1825, a white smith (scurvy, aged 21 years).

Tiernam, Patrick, 25/01/1825, a shoemaker (scurvy, aged 33 years).

Sullivan, Thomas, 18/9/1826, a gardener (scurvy, aged 35 years).

Campbell, Julius, 26/10/1826, an African from Jamaica, a ship steward (speared, aged 34 years.)

Johnson, Henry, 2/12/1826, a servant (scurvy, aged 31 years).

Jepson, Stephen, 7/12/1826, no information (possibly died of fever).

Plomer, Francis, 10/3/1827, a carpenter (fever, aged 25 years,

MARINES

Jenkins, Reece, 16/1/1825, Private Royal Marines (died of tetanus after fracture of the tibia and fibula).

Courtnay, Thomas, 18/5/1825, Private, Royal Marines (scurvy).

Bennett, William, 6/6/1825, Private, Royal Marines (scurvy).

Gwillan, Samuel, 11/6/1825, Corporal, Royal Marines (speared).

Thomas, Richard, 29/8/1825, Private, Royal Marines (unspecified cause).

Burton, William, 11/10/1826, Private, Royal Marines (unspecified cause).

Brookshaw, John, 31/12/1826, Sergeant, Royal Marines (cholera).

SOLDIERS

Hodder, Samuel, 15/3/1825, Private, 3rd Buffs (unspecified cause).

Burley, Thomas, 1/6/1825, Private, 3rd Buffs (unspecified cause).

Flinn, John, 22/11/1825, Private, 3rd Buffs (unspecified cause).

Farrell, George, 20/12/1825, Private, 3rd Buffs (unspecified cause).

Polvine, James, 27/6/1826, Private, 3rd Buffs (unspecified cause).

Calvert, Richard, 2/1/1827, Private, 57th Regiment, (died of fever).[*]

Pembrick, Edward, 6/1/1827, Private, 57th Regiment (died of fever).

Warren, John, 1/2/1827, Private, 57th Regiment (died of fever).

Bailey, John, 3/5/1827, Corporal, 57th Regiment (unspecified cause).

Brown, Patrick, 21/9/1827, Corporal, 57th Regiment (died of food poisoning).

OTHERS

Hicks, Sophie, 2/11/1827, wife of Lieutenant Hicks (died in childbirth).

Hicks, baby girl, 2/11/1827 (died at birth).

Gold, John P., 2/11/1827, Assistant Surgeon (speared).

Green, John Henry, 2/11/1827, a commissary stores officer (speared).

---

[*] The 'fever' was probably malaria, although possibly melioidosis.

APPENDIX 5: LIST OF OTHER SHIPS AT FORT DUNDAS

HMS MERMAID

His Majesty's Ship Mermaid was a colonial cutter constructed of teak in Calcutta, in 1816. She was eighteen metres long, weighed eighty-four tonnes, and carried a single six-pounder gun. Fourteen crew members were required for sail her efficiently. The government in Sydney purchased the *Mermaid* for survey work for £2000. Phillip Parker King used her to explore and chart the north coast of New Holland in 1818, filling in the gaps left by Matthew Flinders. King made three journeys north between 1818 and 1820. He looked for any river 'likely to lead to an interior navigation into this great continent,' and he collected information about topography, fauna and flora, timber, minerals, climate, as well as 'information on the natives and the prospects of developing trade with them.' King made charts of Port Essington and the north coasts of Melville and Bathurst Islands, naming the shoals at the top of the Apsley Strait after his ship.

After the third exploration journey, the *Mermaid* was renovated and converted from a single-masted cutter to a two-mast topsail schooner, which greatly increased her manoeuvrability.

The *Mermaid* was one of the ships, along with the *Lady Nelson* and the *Prince Regent* which Captain Allman used to establish Port Macquarie in April 1821. She was then used for further exploration work, taking John Oxley up the Queensland coast where they discovered and charted the Brisbane River, Moreton Bay, and Stradbroke Island and identified a suitable site for a new convict settlement. With John Oxley was the convict John Richardson, who was to become the gardener on Melville Island, and Stephen Partridge (mentioned only because he is an ancestor of the author).

In 1824, a detachment of the 40th Regiment of Foot and a party of convicts were sent on the *Mermaid* to set up the Moreton Bay Convict Settlement at Redcliffe. This was named in a ceremony twelve days before Bremer named Fort Dundas, although the settlement was moved within a few months to the current site of Brisbane on the river.

In 1825, Governor Darling sent the *Mermaid* to rescue the starving Fort Dundas residents and for the next four years, she made successful victualing runs to Timor and Sydney for both Fort Dundas and Fort Wellington. Her thirteen year career came to an end when her drunken captain, Samuel Nolbrow, ran her onto Franklands Reef, a part of the Great Barrier Reef, in June, 1829, on a high tide with a rising sea. Nolbrow had been carrying orders to Fort Wellington for it to shut down.

HMS ISABELLA/ ESSINGTON

His Majesty's Ship Isabella was a schooner that Captain John Ross used in an unsuccessful search for the North West Passage in 1818. Despite the lack of success, this journey was notable because a new innovation, the canning of food, allowed them to carry and use tinned meat in the stores for the first time.

By 1826, the *Isabella* was in southern waters and she transported Major John Campbell and the soldiers of the 57th Regiment to Fort Dundas to relieve Captain Maurice Barlow and the 3rd Regiment after their two-year posting. The *Isabella* then returned to Sydney with the convicts who had earned their freedom but was to make several runs back to Fort Dundas before 1828. She was used as a transport vessel for several years after that, before being sold into private hands and undergoing a complete renovation, including receiving a new name, *Essington*. She was then posted to Victoria Settlement in the command of Captain Thomas Watson. The *Essington* rescued the British slave, Joseph Forbes (see Chapter 9).

HMS SIR PHILLIP DUNDAS

His Majesty's Ship Sir Phillip Dundas first arrived at Fort Dundas bringing much needed supplies of flour, preserved meat, and pickles in early 1826. On her return to Sydney, she carried news of the dire straits the settlement was in after the loss of the *Lady Nelson*, and this prompted Governor Darling to assign the *Mermaid* to replace her. The *Sir Phillip Dundas* was later the brig which transported Captain Hartley and fresh soldiers from the 57*ᵗʰ* Regiment to Fort Dundas when he relieved Campbell in 1828, and she then returned a number of convicts to Sydney who were too sick to remain.

Later that year, on 19 August 1828, on a journey back to England under the command of Captain Scarvall, she was wrecked during a storm in Algoa Bay, South Africa, with two of her crew drowned.

HMS AMITY

His Majesty's Ship Amity was a two-masted brig, square rigged on both masts, built in Canada in 1816. Weighing 151 tonnes, she was twenty-three metres long and six and a half metres abeam. The New South Wales Government originally purchased the *Amity* in 1824 to aid the new settlement of Moreton Bay and to run supplies to the Norfolk Island convict settlement. Then, in 1827 and 1828, she made a number of trips to Melville Island under the command of Captain Walker, who was accompanied by his wife and children. Whilst moored in King's Cove there was a scandal involving Mrs Walker on board, and the officers of the ship were drawn into serious quarrels with the men. The scandal enraged the Commandant and Mrs Walker was sent ashore with her children and convict servant, Jane Baker (see Chapter 7), because their presence aboard was 'to the detriment of the Public Service'[107].

On her next voyage to Melville Island, in 1828, the Amity was commanded by Captain Owen. Owen is mentioned in the trial of the convict Wilson (see Chapter 7) when Wilson was caught illegally using a dinghy to buy grog from him.

The *Amity* was sold back into private ownership in 1831, and she spent most of the rest of her career based in Hobart operating as a whaler, a sealer, a general carrier and a stock transporter. Then, in 1845, she was sailing from Hobart for Port Albert with Captain William Marr and a crew of nine and one passenger. While they were entering Bass Strait, the weather turned bad and a gale hit the *Amity;* she ran aground southeast of Flinders Island. She was abandoned as she broke up on the rocks, but the crew managed to get to the island safely.

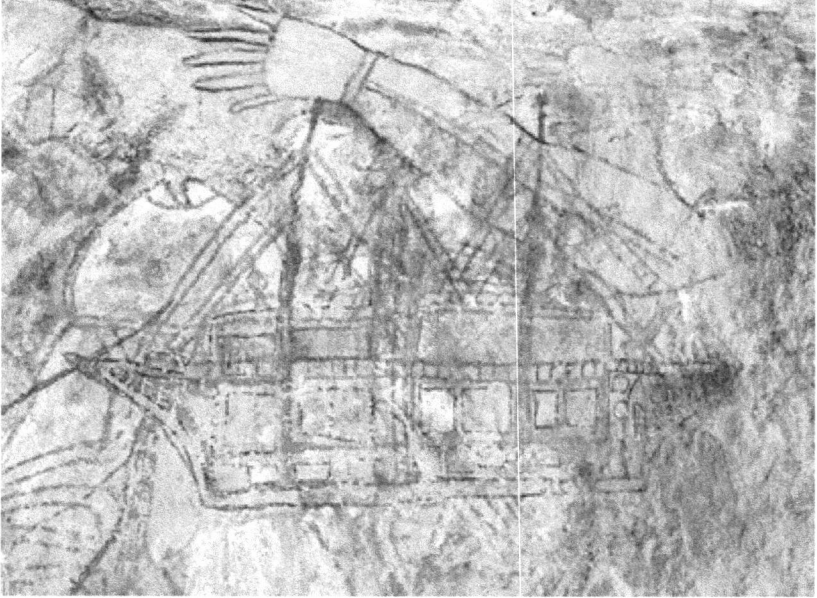

Figure 18 Contact painting: this rock painting near Fort Wellington is thought to represent HMS Amity, HMS Success or a combination of them both.

HMS MARY ELIZABETH

Lieutenant William Hicks commanded *His Majesty's Ship Mary Elizabeth*. She arrived at Port Cockburn to relieve the *Mermaid* in 1827.

Hicks brought his wife Sophie and their son William with him. Sophie was to die in childbirth on the same day that Assistant Surgeon Gold was speared to death (see Chapter 5). She was probably the first European woman to die in north Australia. At that time Hicks was officer in charge at Fort Dundas as Campbell was visiting Fort Wellington.

After the fort closed, Hicks and the *Mary Elizabeth* returned to Sydney in August 1828. He remained in command of the ship for several years, making voyages to Port Macquarie, Moreton Bay and,

174

in 1830, he sailed to the Isle of France to bring back cargo. Hicks was absent from New South Wales for so long he lost his land allotment at Newcastle in 1838.

HMS GOVERNOR PHILLIP

His Majesty's Ship Governor Phillip was a 177-ton government brig built in 1821. She was used mainly to ply the route between Sydney and Norfolk Island. For example, on 22 May 1839, she sailed from Sydney for Norfolk Island carrying cattle, stores, and passengers, including fourteen prisoners and a guard of thirty-four soldiers of the 80th Regiment. She visited Melville Island at least once in 1828, and transported the invalid convicts too weak to last another wet season back to Sydney.

In 1829, the brig transported the soldiers, convicts, and government stores from the closing Fort Wellington to Western Australia. These included Captain Collet Barker and Assistant Surgeon Thomas Wilson[*] who used the *Governor Phillip* as a base to explore the south coast of Western Australia and its hinterland as they passed.

The *Governor Phillip* was sunk on 5 November 1848 after hitting a reef off Gull Island in the Furneaux Group when en route to Hobart. Sixteen crew and passengers were lost, but sixty-nine others were saved (*The Moreton Bay Courier* 16 Dec 1848).

HMS SUCCESS

His Majesty's Ship Success was a 28-gun ship that is most famous for exploring Western Australia and the Swan River in 1827. She was launched in 1825 and was therefore still quite new when she was sent on a mission to Melville Island. She was used for the establishment of the Fort Wellington outpost under the command of Captain James Stirling, who later was the Governor of Western Australia.

The *Success* seems to have made a big impression on at least one Arnhem Land rock artist. In a rock art gallery known as *Djulirri* in North West Arnhem Land, there is a fine painting of a two mastered

---

[*]   See Dr Thomas Wilson's book: *Narrative of a Voyage around the World.*

175

ship such as the *Success*, and although it has been repaired and added to several times, it is possible that this painting was originally of the *Success* and painted about 1827[*] [85].

The *Success* later had an illustrious career in the settlement of the Swan River colony and is fondly remembered in Western Australia by several place names. Her later years were spent as a harbour boat in Portsmouth, until 1849 when she was finally broken up.

THE BRIGS MARCUS AND ANN

These two brigs were used to transport and deliver cargos of buffalos from Timor. They were chartered by the French merchant, Charles Becharde, who was based in Kupang. In 1827, the *Ann* made two trips between Kupang and Port Cockburn, bringing in 151 buffalos and an unknown number of pigs. The *Marcus* arrived in Port Cockburn in September 1828 under the command of Captain Rough with a further fifty seven buffalos. Adding to the three buffalo and the pigs which had arrived earlier these animals were the basis of the feral buffalo and pig population that is now spread across northern Australia.

HMS SLANEY

HMS Slaney 'remained outside, eighteen miles off' when she visited Melville Island and Fort Dundas in 1825. Her captain was unwilling to risk sailing her through the Mermaid Shoals, so he sent in a smaller boat instead - a luxury cargo ships could not take. The Slaney was a man-o-war sloop with twenty guns. She was involved in the Burmese War, in India, and in Jamaica during the 1820s, so must have been passing through when she visited.

HMS LOME

H.M.S. *Lome* was an East Indiaman based in India. She visited Fort Dundas briefly in 1827.

---

[*] The *Amity* was also a two masted vessel. The painting might be one or other, or an amalgamation of several ships.

APPENDIX 6: FORT WELLINGTON, RAFFLES BAY

Fort Wellington has its own history, and as a sister to Fort Dundas, it is worth relating some of it here. The British Government initially planned to have two garrison outposts on the north coast, but Bremer had only enough resources to start a single settlement in 1824. Port Essington was always a preferred site but when the second settlement was finally built, Raffles Bay, a little to the east of Port Essington, was chosen.

The genesis of Fort Wellington appears to have gathered momentum by April 1826. The Earl of Bathurst had read the negative views and reports sent from Fort Dundas and was by then concluding the settlement on Melville Island was unsatisfactory. On 7 April, he instructed Governor Darling to investigate and establish a second settlement on the north coast, east of Melville Island [18].

Governor Darling sent Captain James Stirling to found the new settlement in two ships: the *HMS Success* and the *HMS Mary Elizabeth*, the latter commanded by Lieutenant William Hicks

On board the two ships with Stirling were thirty soldiers of the 39th Regiment of Foot led by the future commandant, Captain H. Smyth, fourteen Marines, and twenty-two convict volunteers.

Stirling chose Raffles Bay after rejecting Croker Island and other possibilities without entering Port Essington. He founded Fort Wellington on 18 June 1827, by raising the flag and firing a salute. Stirling stayed only a short time but went on to greater things as the first governor of the colony of Western Australia.

Major Campbell had been commandant at Fort Dundas for nearly ten months when the new Fort was established, and he might have realised then that he was in command of a settlement that was in the last throes of its existence. Time might have started moving more slowly for the worn out commandant, as he waited for relief, but he made at least one visit to Fort Wellington, which, if nothing else, would have given him a break in the monotony of life on Melville Island.

Fort Wellington didn't do any better than Fort Dundas. Campbell's successor, Captain Hartley, called in at the new fort for a day or two on his way to Melville Island and found it a very sick and depressing place. Within its first year, scurvy hit the settlers hard and Captain Smyth was replaced by Lieutenant Sleeman in April 1828, because he was too sick to continue. Sleeman was himself replaced by the forty-three-year-old Captain Collet Barker* in August 1828.

Barker seems to have been the only commandant in the two northern outposts to have been suited to the role and actually wanted to be there. Under his leadership, the community started to progress quickly. The gardeners grew better food and the health of the populace started to improve. Barker developed good relationships with the local Aboriginal people, the Iwaidja, and he wrote glowing reports of the potential of the settlement. However, these reports were too late to influence anyone as the decision to entirely abandon the north coast had already been taken by Sir George Murray in November 1828. Fort Wellington closed in August 1829, some six months after Fort Dundas, and its stock and stores were transported to the Swan River settlement in Western Australia.

Nowadays at Raffles Bay, there are few signs of the settlement. A few stone foundations of rectangular buildings (which, incidentally, are in better condition than those at Fort Dundas) and several wells can be found in the scrub and, on the rocky beach, there is a straight cutting through the rocks that gave the garrison's small boats access to the sand. Famously, when the settlement was abandoned it was left intact and Barker presented it to an Iwaidja man, who had adopted the name *Wellington*, for his use.

An excellent short history of Fort Wellington can be found in Alan Powell's book, *World's End*.

---

* Barker was an impressive individual. After a posting as commandant of the penal settlement at King George Sound in Western Australia (later closed, ironically, by Governor Stirling because he didn't want convicts in the western colonies), Barker was promoted to be the Resident in the troubled North Island of New Zealand. He never made it there: when travelling to this posting in 1831, he was asked to locate the mouth of the river Murray. While he was exploring Encounter Bay Aboriginal warriors speared him to death on 30 April 1831.

BIBLIOGRAPHY

1. The Age, 1959, *The World's Strangest Stories: The Pirates of Baba*, Melbourne, June 25, 1959.

2. Ainsworth, W., (ed) 1875, *All Around the World: An Illustrated Record of Voyages, Travels and Adventures in all Parts of the Globe*, William Collins, Sons & Co, London, Vol III.

3. Allen, F.J., 1969, *Archaeology and the History of Port Essington*, PhD thesis, Australian National University.

4. Allen, J., 2008, *Port Essington: The Historical Archaeology of a North Australian Nineteenth Military Outpost*, Sydney University Press.

5. The Argus, 1839, *Rescue of a British Subject from the Savages of Timor Laut*, 27 July 1839 Melbourne, Vic.

6. _____, 1938, *In the Clutches of Black Pirates, A True Story of an English Sailor's Sufferings in Timor 100 Years Ago*, Melbourne, Vic., 20 August 1938, http://trove.nla.gov.au/ndp/del/article/12474705.

7. Armstrong, B., 2009, http://www.historyofhomeopathy.com.au/people/item/150-sherwin-dr-william.html.

8. Australian Dictionary of Biography, 1967, *Richardson, John Matthew (1797–1882),* National Centre of Biography, Australian National University. Published first in hardcopy 1967, accessed 14 June 2015.

9. Australian Dictionary of Biography, Bach, J, 1966, *Bremer, Sir James John (1786–1850)*, National Centre of Biography, Australian National University. http://adb.anu.edu.au/biography/bremer-sir-james-john-1823/text2091. Published first in hardcopy 1966, accessed 30 November 2015.

10. The Australian, Anonymous 1825, *Journal of a Gentleman Officer at Fort Dundas 10 March 1825.*

11. Bach, J., 1958, *Melville Island and Raffles Bay, 1824-9, An Unsuccessful Settlement,* Journal of the Royal Historical Society of Australia, 44(4): 233–37.

12. Barns, Capt W., 1823, Letter: *Barns to Earl Bathurst,* 23.7.1823. Colonial Office 201/146.

13. Barlow, Capt M., 1825, Letter: *Barlow to Major Ovens,* Historical Resources of Australia Series III, Volume V, p 644.

14. Barrow, J., 1824, Letter: *Barrow to Horton W (Admiralty),* The National Archives, Kew Colonial Office 201/153, 109028, p 7 ff.

15. _____, 1825, Letter: *Barrow to Horton W (Admiralty),* The National Archives, Colonial Office Kew 201/164, 30.4.1825.

16. Bathurst, Earl, 1824*, Letter: Earl Bathurst to Governor Thomas Brisbane*, Historical Records of Australia, Series 1, Vol. 2, 17 February: pp227–28.

17. _____, 1824, Letter: *Lord Bathurst to the Lords Commissioners of the Admiralty*, Downing Street, The National Archives Kew, ADM 1//4239 109028, Historical Records of Australia Series III, Vol V: 759.

18. _____, 1826, Letter: *Bathurst to Governor Ralph Darling*, HRA Series 1 Vol XII, p 224.

19. Batterby, P., 2007, *To the Islands: White Australia and the Malay Archipelago since 1788*, Lexington.

20. Begbie, J., 1825, Letter: *Begbie to RW Horton,* The National Archives, Kew, Colonial Office 201/166. 109028, p 232.

21. Blainey, G., 1966, *The Tyranny of Distance, How distance Shaped Australia's History*, MacMillan.

22. Blaxland, G., 1972, *The Buffs*, Osprey.

23. Bown, R., 2003, *Scurvy: How a Surgeon, a Mariner and a Gentleman Solved the Greatest Medical Mystery in the Age of Sail*, Viking.

24. Bremer, J.G., 1824, Letter: Bremer to J.W. Croker, Secretary to the Admiralty, Historical Records of Australia, Series 3, Vol. 5, 1922, August and 11 November: 769–80.

25.   _____, 1824, Letter: Bremer to Lord Bathurst, Historical Records of Australia, Series 3, Vol. 5, 1922, 12 November: 785.

26.   _____, 1824, *Captain's log, H.M.S. Tamar*, Public Record Office.

27.   Brisbane, T., 1824, Letter: Brisbane to Earl Bathurst, Historical Records of Australia, Series 3, Vol. 5, 1922, 14 February: 226.

28.   Brock, J., 1993, *Native Plants of North Australia*, Reed.

29.   Calley, G., 2000, *The Pumpkin Settlements, Agriculture and Animals in Australia's First Northern Settlements*, Historical Society of the Northern Territory.

30.   Cameron, J.M.R., 1985, *Traders, Government Officials and the Occupation of Melville Island in 1824*, The Great Circle, 7(2): 88–99.

31.   _____, 1998, *The British meet the Tiwi: Melville Island, 1824'*, in *Connection and disconnection: encounters between settlers and Indigenous people in the Northern Territory*, Tony Austin and Suzanne Parry, (eds.) Darwin, Northern Territory University Press: 27–48.

32.   _____, 2016, *"Stakes in a ring fence', or how John Barrow Secured Australia for the British*, Northern Territory Historical Studies: A Journal of History, Heritage and Archaeology, No 27.

33.   Campbell, J., 1834, *Geographical memoir of Melville Island and Port Essington on the Cobourg Peninsula, Northern Australia; with some observations on the settlements which have been established on the north coast of New Holland*

Journal of the Royal Geographical Society of London, 4: 129-181.

34. _____, 1825, *Attack by Aborigines*, State Record of New South Wales: Copy of Document 245.

35. _____, 1826, Letters: Campbell to Alexander Macleay, Colonial Secretary, Historical Records of Australia, Series III, Vol. VI 1st October: 673; 10 October: p671 and p676; and 20 December, p 681.

36. _____, 1827, Letters: Campbell to Alexander Macleay, Colonial Secretary, Historical Records of Australia, Series III, Vol. V, 1st April: p713; 8th April: p801, p 804; 7th June p 691; 20 June, p721; 29 September, p700; and 9 November: 822–23, and Enclosures, 9 November: 701-705.

37. _____, 1828, Dispatch Number 11: Campbell to Alexander McLeay, Colonial Secretary, Historical Records of Australia Series III, Vol VI, pp 728, .20 June 1828.

38. Cavenagh, C., 1992, *Neither Honour nor Glory: Redcoats on the Northern Coast. The Establishment of Fort Dundas,* Hue and Cry 28, Feb-March 1992.

39. Christie, E.M., 1940, *The Bethel Ship*, The Argus, Melbourne 26 March 1940.

40. Cole, T., 1992 *Riding the Wildman Plains and Crocodiles and Other Characters*, The Tom Cole Omnibus, Macmillan.

41. Collins, David, 1798, *An Account Of The English Colony In New South Wales: With remarks On The Dispositions, Customs, Manners, Etc. Of The Native Inhabitants Of That Country To Which Are Added, Some Particulars Of New Zealand.* http://gutenberg.net.au/.

42. The Colonist, 1839 *Rescue of a British Subject from the Savages of Timor Laut*, 27 July 1839, http://trove.nla.gov.au

43. Connah, G. 1988, *The Archaeology of Australia's History*, CUP.

44. Connor, J., 2002, *The Australian Frontier Wars*, 1788-1838, UNSW Press.

45. Crassweller, C., 2006, *Archaeological Survey of the Proposed Airstrip at Andranangoo Mine Site, Melville Island, NT*, http://www.ntepa.nt.gov.au.

46. Crosby, E., 1975, *Survey and excavation at Fort Dundas, Melville Island, Northern Territory, 1975*, Sydney, The Australian Society for Historical Archaeology.

47. Darling, R., 1828, Letter: Governor Darling to W. Huskisson, Secretary of State, 25 February: Historical Records of Australia, Series 1 Vol. 13, 1920, p794.

48. _____, 1827, Letter: Governor Darling to Viscount Goderich, 13 October 1827, Historical Records of Australia Series 1, Vol 111, pp 549-551.

49. de la Rue, C.J., 2007, *For the Good of His Majesty's Service: The Archaeology of Fort Dundas 1824 – 1829, Masters of Arts by Research Thesis, Charles Darwin University.*

50. Department of Natural Resources, Environment, The Arts and Sport, *A History of Melville Island, Tiwi Islands*, http://www.territorystories.nt.gov.au/.

51. Dowsett, S., 1828, Statement, 709–10, Historical Records of Australia, Series 3, Vol. 6, 1923.

52. Ennis, H., 1825, *Remarks on Board His Majesty's Ship Tamar in a Voyage England to Port Praia, Cape of Good Hope, New South Wales, and thence along the coast of Australia to Port Essington in the Cobourg Peninsula, and thence to Bathurst and Melville Islands, Apsley's Straits, between 27 February and 13th of November, 1824; and continued in the ship Countess of Harcourt, to the Isle of France, to 7 February 1825,* Monthly Magazine, London, 1825, issues 413-417.

53. _____, 1825, *Voyages from England to Australia,* in The Monthly Magazine, #413, August 1, 1825, and #414 September 1, 1825.

54. Evans, N., 1992, '*Macassan loanwords in Top End languages*', Australian Journal of Linguistics, 12(1) June: 45-91.

55. Everard, R., 1826, letter to his sister Fanny, 24 September 1826, Journal of the Buffs Regiment, The Dragon, March 1912. British Museum (cited in Spillett).

56. Flynn, Father Frank, MSC, 1963, *Northern Gateway*, Leonard.

57. Forrest P. & Forrest S., 2005, *Tiwi meet the future: ngawurraningimarri: all come together,* Tiwi Land Council.

58. _____, 2005, *Tiwi meet the Dutch: The First European Contacts,* Tiwi Land Council.

59. Frederickson, C., 2001 *Confinement by Isolation: convict mechanics and labour at Fort Dundas,* Melville Island, Australian Historical Archaeology, 19, 2001 pp4859.

60. _____, 2003, *Archaeology at Fort Dundas, 1975-2000,* Journal of Northern Territory History: No 14, 2003, pp 1-10.

61. Frawley, J., 2003, *People Got a Gun: the 1914 Melville Island Enquiry,* Journal of Northern Territory History: No 14, 2003, pp 51-70.

62. Genealogical Society of the Northern Territory, www.pastmasters.net.

63. Goodale, J.C., 1982, Tiwi Wives: A Study of the Women of Melville Island, North Australia, Ann Arbor University Microfilms, Michigan.

64. Grassby, A., and Hill, M., 1988, *Six Australian battlefields,* North Ryde, Angus and Robertson.

65. Hart, C., and Pilling, A., 1960, *The Tiwi of North Australia*, Holt, Rinehart and Winston.

66. Hartley, H.R., 1828, Letter: Captain Hartley to Colonial Secretary McLeay, Melville Island, Historical Records of Australia, Series 3, Vol. 4 pp 715-720, 12 May 1828.

67. _____, 1828, Letter: Hartley to Alexander Macleay, Colonial Secretary, Historical Records of Australia, Series 3, Vol. 5, 8 September pp760-763.

68. Hay, R.W., 1826, Letter: Hay to Barrow, 6 April 1826, Historical Resources of Australia Series 1, Vol XII, pp 224-225.

69. Hill, E., 1951, *The Territory*, Sydney, Angus and Robertson.

70. Historical Records of Australia, 1824, Aug 23, *Agreement to go to the new settlement at Melville Island* Reel 6066; 4/1802 pp.17-20.

71. Hobart Town Gazette and Van Diemen's Land Advertiser (Tasmania 1821 - 1825).

72.   Hobart Town Courier, *Early Hunter Valley Settlers* reference from 1828, www.jenwilletts.com/william_hicks.

73.   Horton, R., 1825, Letter: *Horton to Barns,* The National Archives Kew, Colonial Office, 202/11 109028, p169.

74.   Howard, D., 1933, *The English activities on the north coast of Australia in the first half of the nineteenth century*, Proceedings of the Royal Geographical Society of Australasia, South Australian Branch, Session 1931-32, 33: 21–194.

75.   King, Philip Parker, 1827, *Narrative of a survey of the intertropical and western coasts of Australia performed between the years 1818 and 1822.* London, John Murray, 1827.

76.   King, Z., 2009, *Watercrafting: A Maritime Archaeological Analysis of three Australian Indigenous Canoes.* Thesis submitted to Flinders University 2009.

77.   Kolff, D.H., 1825-26, Voyages of the Dutch Brig of War *Dourga* (Translated by GW Earl, London, 1840, in Lee, 1915).

78.   Larpent, G.G. de H., 1825, Letter to RJ Wilmot Horton, 17 May 1825, Colonial Office Records, CO201/176.

79.   Laws, Captain, 1828, *Report on the Settlements of Northern Coast of Australia*, The National Archives Kew CO 201/264 PP51-55. See Street 2012.

80.   Lee, I., 1915, *The Log Books of the Lady Nelson* http// standardlibrary. com/authors/l/ida_lee/00007509. Accessed August 2016.

81.   Lewis H.J., 1914, *The President's Annual Address*, Royal Geographical Society of Australia, South Australian Branch, 28*th* Session.

82. Lockwood, D., 1968, *The Front Door*, Adelaide, Rigby.

83. Macquarie, Lachlan, 1822, *Diary, 11 March 1821 - 12 February 1822*. Mitchell Library, Sydney. www.mq.edu.au/macquarie-archive/journeys/ships/list. Accessed August 2016.

84. Marshall, H., 1991, *Convict pioneers and the failure of the management system of Melville Island, 1824-29*, Push 29: 29-46.

85. May, S., Paul, S., Taçon, D., and Pearson, M., 2013, *Painted ships on a Painted Arnhem Land Landscape*, The Great Circle, Vol 31 No 2.

86. McInnis, A., 1983, *The Wreck of the 'Charles Eaton'*, Royal Historical Society of Queensland, 24 February 1983, www.espace.library.uq.edu.au.

87. McIntosh, A., 1958, *Early Settlement in North Australia*, Medical Journal of Australia 1(13) 1958.

88. Meston, A., 1914, *Australia's Largest Island*, Sydney Morning Herald, 1 May.

89. Miller, G., 1825, Letter to Captain Barlow 9 Feb 1825, Colonial Office Records, CO201/176.

90. *Monthly Magazine or British Register*, Vol LX part II, 1825 p302.

91. Morris, J., 1964, *Relationship between the British and the Tiwi in the vicinity of Fort Dundas, Melville Island*, read to the Historical Society of the Northern Territory, 26 October.

92. _____, 1971, An outline of the history of the settlement

at Fort Wellington, Raffles Bay, N.T., in *Fort Wellington, Raffles Bay, North Australia*, Historical Society of the Northern Territory, Darwin: 14–40.

93. _____, 2001, *The Tiwi and the British: an ill-fated outpost.* Aboriginal History, Vol 25. Pp 243-261. ANU Press.

94. _____, 1999, *The Tiwi: from Isolation to Cultural Change*, MA thesis, University of Ballarat, April.

95. Mundle, R., 2014, *The First Fleet*, ABC Books.

96. Muller, J., 1746, *A Treatise Containing the Elementary Part of Fortification, Regular and Irregular*, Museum Restoration Service, Ottawa, Ontario, quoted from de la Rue, 2007 *For the Good of His Majesty's Service: The Archaeology of Fort Dundas 1824 – 1829, Masters of Arts by Research Thesis, Charles Darwin University.*

97. Mountford, C.P., 1959, '*Expedition to the land of the Tiwi*', The National Geographic Magazine, 109 (3), March: 417–40.

98. Murray, Sir G., 1828, Letter: Murray to Governor Darling 1 November 1829: Historical Resources of Australia Series 1 Vol XIV p 410.

99. _____, 1829, Letter: Murray to Governor Darling 15 May 1829: Colonial Office 714/118. No 79915.

100. Northern Territory News 1974, '*First Settlement. 150th Anniversary*', 20 September: 13–18.

101. NSW Government Gazette, July 5th 1837, *Certificates of Freedom.* http://gazette.slv.vic.gov.au/images/1837/N/general/283.pdf. Accessed August 2016.

102. http://www.pastmasters.net/fort-dundas-et-al.html.

103. Parsons, H.A., 1907, *The Truth About the Northern Territory*, Adelaide: Hussey and Gillingham.

104. Pasco, C., 1886, *An Account of the Rescue of Joe Forbes from Timor Laut in 1839*. A paper read to the Historical Society of Australasia, 3rd September 1886.

105. Pearn, J., and Carter P., (Eds), 1995, *Islands of Incarceration*, Australian Society for the History of Medicine, Amphion Press.

106. Port Macquarie Historical Society (1996) *Port Macquarie The Winding Sheet: The Burying Grounds, 1921-1886*. PMHS.

107. Powell, A., 1988, *Far Country*, (2nd ed.), Carlton: Melbourne University Press.

108. _____, 2010, *Northern Voyages: Australia's Monsoon Coast in Maritime History*, Australian Scholarly Publication.

109. _____, 2016, *'World's End: British Military Outposts in the 'Ring Fence' around Australia, 1824-1849*, Australian Scholarly Publication.

110. Pye, J., 1977, *The Tiwi*, Coleman.

111. Reid B., 1995, Melville Island: Convict outpost and the first colonial settlement in northern Australia, in *Islands of Incarceration*, J. Pearn and P. Carter (eds), Australian Society for the History of Medicine, Amphion Press.

112. Reynolds, H., 1978, *Aboriginal-European Contact History: problems and issues*, Journal of Australian Studies, 3: 52–64.

113. Risby, W., *The Lady Nelson,* www.tasfamily.net.au.

114. Roe, J. S., 1824, *John Septimus Roe letters, the experienced navigator returns to Australian waters: The voyage of the Tamar 15 February 1824 - 18 July 1825*, Series 07 http://acms.sl.nsw.gov.au/.

115. _____, 1824, Letter, John Septimus Roe to James Roe HM Ship Tamar at Sea, Lat 16° S Long 113°E, 29 November: 2–3.

116. _____, 1824, Letter, John Septimus Roe to John Piper, HM Ship Tamar at Sea, 7 December 1824, Piper Correspondence.

117. Russell, Henry S., 1888, *The Genesis of Queensland : an account of the first exploring journeys to and over Darling Downs, the earliest days of their occupation, social life, station seeking, the course of discovery, northward and westward, and a resume of the causes which led to separation from New South Wales, with portrait and facsimiles of maps, log etc. etc.* Turner & Henderson, 1888.

118. Sargent, C., 1995, *The Buffs in Australia – 1822 to 1827*, Sabretache (Military Historical Society of Australia), XXXVI (January/March: 3-13

119. _____, 1996, *The Colonial Garrison, 1817-24: The 48th Foot, The Northamptonshire Regiment in the Colony of New South Wales*, TCS Publications, Canberra.

120. Scott, E., 2002, *A Short History of Australia*, University of Melbourne 0200471h.html.

121. Searcy, A., 1905, *In Northern Seas*, WK Thomas and Co, Adelaide.

122. _____, 1909, *In Australian Tropics*, London, George Robertson.

123. Smyth, H., 1827, Captain Smyth to Colonial Secretary Macleay, Despatch No 3 per HMS Success. Historical Records of Australia, Series III, Vol VI.

124. State Records of NSW *Attack by Aborigines* COD 245, Report on Julius Campbell's death.

125. Statham, P., 1989, *The Origins of Australia's Capital Cities*, Cambridge University Press

126. Stotz, C.M., 1958, 'Defence in the Wilderness', in *Drums in the Forest*, Vol 1, James, A.P., and Stotz, C.M. (Eds.) The Historical Society of Pennsylvania page 132.

127. Spillett, P., 1980, *Final Report of Fellowship Program January 1980 – May 1980*, Report to Churchill Fellowship copy held in Northern Territory State Library.

128. _____, 1974, *The First Settlement at Fort Dundas*, Darwin Shopper, 11/9/74: 4, 8.

129. _____, 1974, *150th Anniversary of First Settlement in Northern Australia: Fort Dundas, Melville Island, 1824 – 1974, A brief account of the early settlements of North Australia from 1824 and a Programme of Events during the Week of Celebrations 22nd – 28th September 1924*, Historical Society of Northern Australia.

130. _____, 1982, *The Discovery of the Relics of HM Colonial Brig Lady Nelson and the Schooner Stedcombe*. Historical Society of the Northern Territory, Darwin.

131. _____, 1983, *From the other side: Indonesian evidence on the loss of the 'Lady Nelson' and 'Stedcombe' (1825)*, The Great Circle, 5(1): 24–39.

132. Street, E., 2012, *Distant Settlements: convicts in remote Australia: biographical details of the convict mechanics who served at the settlements of Melville Island (1824-1829), Raffles Bay (1827-1829), Western Port (1826-1827) and King George's Sound (1827-1830)*, editor Brian Reid, Darwin Historical Society.

133. Sydney Gazette, and New South Wales Advertiser (NSW 1803 - 1842).

134. _____, 1825, *Extracts from the journal of 'An Officer of the Expedition'* 10 March 1825, http://trove.nla.gov.au. Accessed August 2016.

135. _____, 20 July 1839, Forbes Rescued, Ship News: http://trove.nla.gov.au/ndp/del/article/2539731. Accessed August 2016.

136. *The Monthly Magazine,* No 413, 1825.

137. Tiwi Land Council, 2001, *A History of Melville Island, Tiwi Islands* http://www.territorystories.nt.gov.au, p11-12. Accessed August 2016.

138. Turner, C., Dr, 1825, Letter: *Assistant Surgeon Turner to Major Ovens, 25 May 1825*, Historical Records of Australia Series III, Vol VI, p650.

139. Warre, Lieutenant-Gen H.J., 1878, *Historical Records Of The Fifty-Seventh, Or, West Middlesex Regiment Of Foot: Compiled From Official And Private Sources, From The Date Of Its Formation In 1755, To The Present Time, 1878; With Preface And Epitome, Together With The Services Of The Honorary Colonels And Lieutenant-Colonels Commanding, And Appendix By The Editor:* Mitchell & Co, London.

140. Watson, P., 2014, *Border Security Australia – 1825 style (includes pirates!)* paulwatson.blogspot.com.au/2014/11.

141. Watson, T., Captain, 1939, *Captain's Log of the Essington*, Corpus of Australia, https://www.ausnc.org.au/corpora/cooee/2-206-raw.

142. The West Australian, 1899, *An Aged Vessel: HMS Success*, 4 May.

143. Wilson, H.D., 1894, The Northern Territory, in *The Province of South Australia*, ed. J.D. Woods, Adelaide, C.E. Bristow, Government Printer: 415–46.

144. Woolfe, R., 2001, *Fort Dundas, First Settlement in Northern Australia*, Final Report for SES440, http://www.territorystories.nt.gov.au/bitstream/handle/10070/230295 accessed August 2016.

Index

ALSO BY DEREK PUGH

A Visiting Teacher in Arnhem Land

reflective,

tragic,

hilarious

Turn Left
at the
Devil Tree

Derek Pugh

Foreword by
Ted Egan AO

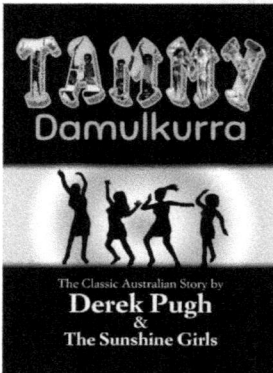

www.ingramcontent.com/pod-product-compliance
Lightning Source LLC
Chambersburg PA
CBHW060023100426
42740CB00010B/1574